KENSINGTON

past and present

View from Kensington Park
Photo by Paul Lettieri

Printed in the United States.
ISBN: 0-942627-76-8
Library of Congress Card Catalog Number: 00-102960

KENSINGTON
past and present

KENSINGTON IMPROVEMENT CLUB

BOARD OF DIRECTORS

OFFICERS: Lorraine Osmundson, *President*; Linda Lipscomb, *Vice-President*; Anthony Knight, *Treasurer*; David Hertzer, *Secretary*

DIRECTORS: Paul Lettieri, Linda Lipscomb, Marianne Loring *(Past President)*, John McKenna, Gloria Morrison, Jaima Roberts, Natalie Salsig *(Past Vice-President)*, Lawrence Thal, Katherine Trow, Martin Trow

EDITORS

Natalie Salsig
Marianne Loring • Katherine Trow

PHOTOGRAPHS

Louis L. Stein
Theodore Osmundson
Paul Lettieri
Natalie Salsig
Katherine Trow
Richard Edwards

LAYOUT & FORMAT

Paul Lettieri

WOODFORD PRESS

Emeryville, California

COVER & BOOK DESIGN

Jim Santore

EDITORIAL ASSISTANCE

Nikki Bruno

This book is dedicated to
all the many volunteers who over the years
have contributed to building the community of Kensington

" . . . To be attached to the subdivision, to love the little platoon we belong to in society is the first principle . . . of public affections . . . the first link in the series by which we proceed toward a love of our country and of mankind. . . ."
—-Edmund Burke, 1790

KENSINGTON
past and present

CONTENTS

Kensington, California

Legend

1. Unitarian Universalist Church
2. Carmelite Monastery
3. U.C. Blake House and Gardens
4. Arlington Community Church
5. Kensington Hilltop School
6. Kensington Community Center
7. Kensington Park
8. Kensington Library
9. Annex and Recreation Office
10. Sunset View Cemetery
11. Sunset Mausoleum
12. EBMUD Filter Plant
13. Public Safety Building
14. Arlington Shopping Center
15. EBMUD Summit Reservoir
16. Colusa Circle Shopping Area

SCALE 0   400

N

CITY OF BERKELEY

FOREWORD

This book was compiled and published by the Kensington Improvement Club (KIC) assisted by dedicated volunteers from the community. It is a tangible representation of the spirit of volunteerism and public service which infuses this community and which has given Kensington a reputation for being a very special place in which to live.

The KIC, first organized in 1921, is the oldest volunteer organization in Kensington. Its mission from the beginning has been to promote and foster the welfare of Kensington, to serve as a liaison between the community and Contra Costa County governmental agencies, to carry out community improvements, and to sponsor an annual town hall meeting at which community issues are discussed.

By working with the County, the KIC has promoted legislation which has been of benefit to the community such as the tree-view ordinance, an ordinance for road improvement, and a second unit ordinance. The KIC has also been instrumental in the formation of the Kensington Municipal Advisory Council (KMAC). In addition, the KIC initiated the undergrounding of utilities and installation of new street lights on Arlington Avenue and at Colusa Circle, and the installation of the Colusa Circle traffic island.

Over the years, the Club has sponsored numerous improvement projects within the community such as the planting along Arlington Avenue and the construction and supervision of the kiosk and the community signboard at the south end of Arlington. The KIC has assisted the community in preparing for emergencies through the publication and distribution of an earthquake preparedness manual and by organizing the Neighborhood Emergency Preparedness program, predecessor to the current Neighborhood Emergency Assistance Team program. To keep abreast of current issues, the Club also monitors the Board meetings of Kensington's special districts.

This book is the third in a series published by the KIC regarding Kensington. Earlier editions, published in 1966 and 1978, were titled *A Survey of Kensington*. In this year of the new millennium, we are taking the community on a tour of *Kensington, Past and Present*.

It is our hope that this book will stimulate interest in the rich history of our area, and that the research that has gone into its writing will help preserve for posterity not only information on the development of our community but also how, through the dedicated efforts of its early volunteers, Kensington coped with and found solutions to the myriad of problems it has faced as a result of being left an unincorporated community in 1917. Through the creative efforts of these volunteers, a solid foundation was formulated which would provide a basis for establishing local control over Kensington's affairs and most of its major services. Building on this foundation, Kensington has been able to succeed in holding onto its village tradition while inevitably evolving into a small urban town. We hope that the text will help clarify the often complicated relationship among the elected boards, councils, clubs, and associations that govern, administer, and conduct the business of the community.

The editors wish to thank those who have given so generously of their time and expertise to make this book possible. Special credit is due to KIC Board member Paul Lettieri for the extensive computer work necessary to prepare the book for publication. Our appreciation is also extended to Janet Wright, daughter of Louis Stein, who gave permission for her father's photographs of early Kensington to be used to illustrate this book, to Madeline Kingsley for her research and her willingness to help computerize the text, and to Claire Wasser for her capable editing.

Further recognition is due to volunteer contributors Renee Benoit, Celia Concus, Carol Krane, Robert Oswalt, and Dolores Prescott and to former KIC Board members Rosemary Barnwell for her work on "Natural Setting," Les Burnett for his research on "Chronology," Ann Maria Celona for her contribution to the section on Kensington's commercial development, and to Joan Gallegos for her work on the section describing emergency preparedness.

Current Board members who contributed to the book include David Hertzer who researched "The People of Kensington," Anthony Knight who tabulated the Questionnaire returns, Lorraine Osmundson who contributed to the Introduction, Jaima Roberts who researched "Schools," Lawrence Thal who researched "Government and Public Services," and Martin Trow who chaired the organizational meetings preliminary to writing the book and contributed to "The People of Kensington." We thank them all, for without their research and expertise this book would not have been possible.

—The Editors

Marianne Loring

Natalie Salsig

Katherine Trow

INTRODUCTION

This book has been prepared by the Kensington Improvement Club for the use and enjoyment of Kensington residents, and for all others who have an interest in the community. This is the third such report. Earlier booklets were published by the Improvement Club in 1966 and 1978; now, two decades later, it is time to bring the story of Kensington up to date.

It is, on the whole, a happy story, for Kensington, California is truly a blessed place. Of course there is room for improvement, as the name of our organization asserts; this book will draw attention to some areas where improvements can be made. Yet Kensington is an exceptional place, and its residents consider themselves fortunate to live here. There can hardly be a more beautiful natural setting for a community. From their homes high on the hills overlooking San Francisco Bay, many residents enjoy a view of one of the most inspiring urban landscapes (and seascapes) in the world, one that thousands of tourists come to see every year.

Kensington lies almost directly opposite the Golden Gate to the west. The Golden Gate Bridge is one of three bridges crossing the sparkling waters of the northern San Francisco Bay. To the southwest are the hills and towers of San Francisco, connected to the east side of the Bay by the San Francisco-Oakland Bay Bridge. To the northwest, the Richmond-San Rafael Bridge leads to Marin County with Mt. Tamalpais visible on the horizon. To the south of Kensington are the communities of Albany, Berkeley and Oakland. To the north and west some of us can see the cities of El Cerrito, Richmond, and San Pablo. From parts of the community we can see San Pablo Bay, and, on a clear day, all the way to Mt. St. Helena to the north. Homes situated at the very top of the hill facing east look out over the undeveloped sweep of Wildcat Canyon and Tilden Regional Parks, with Mount Diablo rising in the distance.

Kensington is not just a living postcard. Perhaps of greater importance to those of us who live here, it is an oasis of peace and serenity in a noisy and harried world. It is, for the most part, a residential community — though we will be describing its two small but lively and important commercial areas. It is a city of detached homes, front lawns, and back gardens — graced and threatened by the raccoons, squirrels, and deer who live among us and thrive on our roses. There are no manufacturing establishments to foul the air, and no shopping malls or entertainment centers to clog the streets. All of that in plenty is just down the hill or across the Bay. Here the air is still clear, the streets mostly quiet. Kensington's neighborliness helps its residents feel they are not alone in the event of emergencies such as an earthquake or fire. Members of the police and fire departments know the small community well, patrol our streets to deter crime, and are always ready to give aid in fire and medical emergencies.

Residents know the pleasures and attractions of Kensington; indeed, that is probably why they live here. Still, this book may reveal some things about the community not everyone knows. After a chronology of historical developments in the area, our story starts with an account of the natural setting of Kensington, of the land as it was and as it is; something of who was here before we came; something of the place through the eyes of a geographer and a botanist.

The next chapter talks about Kensington in historical times. It has a rich history as a community, even if a relatively short one. And we have the help of a wonderful archive of photographs of old Kensington to illustrate the story of its founding and growth. We then turn to a discussion of the community as it is today — its distinctive qualities, its architecture and real estate.

The book goes on to describe Kensington's commercial community, both the shops and the stores in the two small business districts and the much wider variety of commercial and professional activities conducted out of people's homes — an increasingly important part of the life of the community as the computer, modem, and Internet make home-based businesses common and practical.

A major section of the book describes Kensington's public services — to many residents the most mysterious aspect of life in Kensington. That may be because as an "unincorporated area" it has so little formal government. This section tries to answer the questions: What is an unincorporated area, why is Kensington organized that way, and how does it provide vital public services such as the police and fire departments? If there is so little formal government, how does anything get done? The answers are neither obvious nor final.

Every community has a variety of needs for public services and decisions. For Kensington, some of these services are provided by local special districts and some by county and other public agencies. For example, the West Contra Costa Unified School District operates Kensington Elementary School, Contra Costa County is responsible for maintaining roads, and the East Bay Regional Park District controls the park just to the east of us. Thus the community has links to many political entities located outside Kensington.

At the same time Kensington residents support and depend upon a variety of volunteer civic organizations, of which the Kensington Improvement Club is one. These groups carry out many of the functions of study and recommendations, and even some actions, which in other communities are the responsibility of city or county governments. A section of the book describes these voluntary activities, surprising to many in their number and variety.

No one who lives in Kensington is very far from the Hayward Fault, or from the chaparral and forests of Wildcat Canyon and Tilden Park from which fierce fires can spread to populated parts of the hills when the wind and weather are right. Recently, and especially since the Loma Prieta earthquake of 1989 and the great Oakland Fire of 1991, people in Kensington, through the Emergency Preparedness Council and the Neighborhood Emergency Assistance Team program, have been preparing for possible disasters. A section of this book reports on those activities, how Kensington has planned and prepared for emergencies, and what remains to be done.

One chapter is devoted to the schools in Kensington, both public and private, and the organizations that support them. Another chapter is about demographic characteristics of the people who live in Kensington, some of it based on information in the U.S. Census and the County Assessor's office.

The book is enriched with maps, charts, illustrations, and a wonderful selection of early photographs taken over the years by the late former resident Louis Stein. We have used information from a four-page questionnaire mailed to all Kensington homes to get a better picture of who lives in Kensington, their ages, where they work, and their views and concerns about various aspects of life in Kensington.

We hope this book will give as much pleasure to its readers as it has to its compilers, and that it will be of use to all.

KENSINGTON CHRONOLOGY

1772 The Pedro Fages Mapping Expedition passed through the Kensington area on its way from what is now El Cerrito to Wildcat Canyon. The area along the East Bay that includes Kensington was inhabited at the time by the Huchiun tribe of Indians who spoke a Costanoan language.

1823 The newly independent government of Mexico granted the San Pablo Rancho to Francisco María Castro.

1826 Francisco María Castro retired from the Mexican army, and he and his family built their first home in the Alvarado Creek area.

1831 Francisco María Castro died, leaving one-half of his estate to his widow Gabriela Berryessa Castro. One twenty-second of his estate went to each of his eleven children. The southern portion, including Kensington, went to Victor, the youngest son.

1838 Jesús María, another of Francisco Castro's sons, built a new adobe home for his widowed mother, Gabriela, at what is now the corner of Church Lane and San Pablo Avenue in San Pablo. Gabriela's daughter, Martina, married California Governor Juan Bautista Alvarado in 1839, and she and her husband moved into the adobe with her mother. On Gabriela's death, in 1851, all her holdings were willed to Martina and her husband.

1839 Victor Castro built a hacienda for his family on the present site of El Cerrito Plaza.

1848 California was ceded to the

Discovery Route of Fages Expedition, March 27-31, 1772

United States. The state constitution was approved in 1849, and on September 9, 1850, California became a state.

1850 Contra Costa County was formed by an act of the State Legislature as one of the original 27 counties.

1853 Alameda County was formed by an act of the State Legislature. Cerrito Creek marked the boundary between the two counties.

1891 The Summit Reservoir at the corner of Spruce Street and Grizzly Peak Boulevard was built. A roof was added to the reservoir in 1972.

1892 Anson Blake bought a portion of Rancho San Pablo, much of which lay in the Kensington area.

1896 A court decision was reached on holdings of the original Castro land grant. Attorney George Leviston was awarded Lot #1 (600 acres) in Kensington in lieu of fees.

St James's Gardens in the Royal Borough of Kensington, London, England   Photo by Katherine Trow

1900 Victor Castro died, and his property went to his many heirs.

1901 George Shima (originally Kinji Ushijima), known as the "Japanese Potato King" because he held thousands of acres of rich potato land in the San Joaquin Valley, bought ten acres bordering Cerrito Creek east of the present day Arlington shopping area.

1906 The San Francisco earthquake and fire brought many people into the East Bay area.

1910 George Leviston sold Lot #1 in Kensington to speculators.

1911 The name "Kensington" was given to the area by Robert Bousefield, one of the two original surveyors, who named

The Amherst Avenue Archway, 1911-1938   Photo by Louis L. Stein

the land after South Kensington, the London borough in which he lived.

A large ornate archway over Amherst Avenue at Arlington Avenue was constructed by Meikle, Brock, and Skidmore of the Berkeley Investment Company as an entrance to their Berkeley Highlands sub-division. It was removed in 1938.

The Kensington Park subdivision west of Arlington Avenue at Ardmore and Coventry Roads was started by Dodge, Ver Mehr of the North End Land Company.

The Berkeley Park subdivision near Colusa Circle was started by Eugene L. Brock of the Berkeley Investment Company.

1912 The Oakland Traction Company extended its street car line up the Arlington to just beyond the Kensington-Berkeley border. Tracks were laid by developers Meikle, Brock, and Skidmore. The "Kensington Park" terminus was on the west side of the Arlington.

Caudron House (at 264 Arlington), which later became Fellowship House, was built as a residence and real estate office for the Berkeley Investment Company.

1913 Berkeley Highlands was opened for development by Meikle, Brock, and Skidmore.

The Stege Sanitary District was formed.

1914 Berkeley Highland Terrace was developed by the F. R. Peake Company.

1917 El Cerrito was incorporated. The boundaries were set for political considerations to exclude Kensington, leaving Kensington as an unincorporated area.

Newspaper Advertisement for Kensington Park
Photo by Louis L. Stein

1919   George Baxter developed Arlington Acres subdivision and founded Sunset View Cemetery.

1920   The population of Kensington was 226.

The Berkeley Woods subdivision, Blakemont area, and property owned by architect Bernard Maybeck were opened for development.

1921   The Kensington Improvement Club (KIC) was organized as the first volunteer group in Kensington.

The East Bay Municipal Utilities District (EBMUD) filter plant was constructed adjacent to Sunset View Cemetery. It was enlarged in 1947.

1922   Harriet Blake and two of her sons with their families moved to Kensington and established the Blake Estate and Gardens.

Electrical and gas lines were brought in by Pacific Gas & Electric Company, and the first street lights were installed.

1923   Many people who were displaced from their homes by the fire in Berkeley became Kensington residents.

1925   The first Kensington Elementary School was opened, and the Kensington PTA was organized.

1926   The George Friend Company opened the Arlington Estates subdivision.

1927   The Mausoleum was constructed on the grounds of the Sunset View Cemetery.

Kensington Fire Department, 1927-1970
Photo by Louis L. Stein

The first youth group, a Boy Scout troop, was sponsored by the Improvement Club. By 1931 Troop 14 had eight boys enrolled.

The Neighborhood Center was built where the present Chevron service station stands at 304 Arlington. It consisted of a firehouse, Hertneck's Grocery, Roy Sulligar's real estate office, and Fred Wallis' gas station.

1928

1928 The Kensington Fire Department was established. It was staffed by volunteers. Fred Wallis became the first fire chief.

The one-acre gore (triangular) lot between Arlington and Amherst Avenues owned by George Shima was sold to Raymond Price, who constructed the commercial building housing Louis Stein's Arlington Pharmacy (299 Arlington).

1930 The population of Kensington was 1,423.

The Machell Police Patrol serviced the Kensington area.

Stores were added north of the Pharmacy.

1932 Arlington Community Church opened Fellowship House in the former Caudron House at 264 Arlington Avenue. John H. Gregg was the first director. Fellowship House became the first community center.

Original Neighborhood Center, 1927-Early 1950s
Photo by Louis L. Stein

1934 John Gregg advertised in a small neighborhood paper (*The Argos*) for interested women to meet at Fellowship House to form the Arlington Women's Club.

1935 Fred Norton was the first paid policeman. He received $1.00 to $1.50 per month from each Kensington household. He furnished his own automobile, a Model T Ford.

Standard Oil Company bought property in the Neighborhood Center at 304 Arlington Avenue.

1936 A very small Young's Market opened at 291 Arlington Avenue, the present location of Dr. Lawrence Thal's optometry office.

1937 The Kensington Fire Department was made an Independent Special District by an act of the State Legislature.

1938   Leon Young constructed a new building for Young's Market at its present location.

1940   The Arlington Variety Store opened to the north of the Pharmacy at 295 Arlington, the present site of Arlington Wine and Spirits.

The Kensington Nursery School opened.

The population of Kensington was 3,355.

1942   El Cerrito Junior-Senior High School was built.

1944   The *Arlington Outlook* was started as a volunteer service project. The Reverend Mr. Herbert Dimock of the Arlington Community Church was the first editor. The "outlook" from his window, a view of the Golden Gate bridge, was his inspiration for the title.

1945   The land for the new Arlington Community Church at Arlington Avenue and Rincon Road was purchased from Anson Blake.

1946   The Kensington Police Protection District was formed.

1948   The Arlington Community Church moved to its new site at 52 Arlington Avenue.

The Community Center Council was formed.

The street car line on Arlington Avenue was replaced by bus service.

Noel Sullivan bought the "pink mansion" from the Blake Estate for a Carmelite Monastery.

1949   The police were equipped with their first official police cars; they no longer had to use their own automobiles.

Arlington Community Church
Photo by Theodore Osmundson

1950

1950   The Arlington Community Church was expanded and continued to serve as Kensington's Community Center.

Arlington Avenue was widened and improved. The street car tracks were removed.

The population of Kensington was 6,601.

A new Kensington Elementary School was built up the hill from the original school. The school enrollment was so large there were six kindergarten classes.

1951   The first volunteer-directed summer recreation program was started by the Community Center Council (which later became the Kensington Community Council) at the Arlington Community Church, under the direction of Mrs. William Stiles.

1952   Kensington hired its first paid firefighters. The Volunteer Firefighters Association continued to augment the service.

1953   The Police Protection District was reorganized as the Kensington Community Services District (KCSD).

1955   The Youth Hut, later renamed the Kensington Community Center, was built, largely with volunteer services.

Responsibility for Parks and Recreation was vested in the KCSD by Kensington voters.

The building at 267 Arlington Avenue which houses medical, dental, and other offices was built by Louis Stein.

1956   The Recreation Advisory Board was established to advise and assist the Community Services District Board of Directors.

Annexation to the city of El Cerrito was voted down by a margin of almost two to one.

Victor Castro's original adobe hacienda, on the present site of the El Cerrito Plaza, burned to the ground.

1957   A drop-in program for teenagers was established at the Youth Hut.

An effort to incorporate Kensington was unsuccessful.

The Blake Estate was donated to the University of California, with the house in trust until the deaths of the elderly Mr. and Mrs. Anson Blake.

1959   On December 17, Kensington became an official postal designation, with positive repercussions for the finances of local service districts. DMV fees and property assessments from Kensington 94707 and 94708 ceased being credited to Alameda County and were credited, instead, to Contra Costa County. Limited postal services were made available at the Arlington Pharmacy.

The Friends of the Kensington Library was organized and incorporated as a non-profit organization.

1960   The Kensington Community Council (KCC) was incorporated, replacing the Community Center Council. The KCC assumed publication of the *Outlook* (formerly named the *Arlington Outlook*).

The population of Kensington was 6,161.

Unitarian Universalist Church
Photo by Theodore Osmundson

1961   Construction of the First Unitarian Church of Berkeley at 1 Lawson Road was completed on land that had been donated by architect Bernard Maybeck.

1962   A new year-round recreation program with an office on the grounds of the lower school south of the Youth Hut was established through the cooperative efforts of the KCC and KCSD.

Plans to replace the original Kensington library housed in the basement of the Arlington Community Church with a

Architectural Elevation of Library

1962

new and larger Kensington branch of the Contra Costa County Library system were approved by Friends of the Kensington Library (FKL).

1963   A library service district was established to finance the new library building.

The KCC drew up a master plan for a recreation area.

1965   The new library building at 61 Arlington Avenue was dedicated.

1966   Kensington residents turned down annexation to El Cerrito for a second time.

The KIC published the first edition of the *Survey of Kensington*.

An amphitheater was added to Kensington Park, behind the Youth Hut. It was designed by Ted Osmundson, who also supervised its construction.

1967   Bonds were passed to bring Kensington school buildings up to earthquake standards.

Amphitheater at the Youth Hut
Photo by Theodore Osmundson

1969   Bonds were passed to build a new public safety building at 217 Arlington Avenue.

Charles J. Hitch was the first President of the University of California to occupy Blake House.

1970   The new public safety building was dedicated.

The mortgage on the library was paid off five years after completion of the building.

The population of Kensington was 5,823.

The original Tot Lot was opened behind the library.

1972   The Kensington Property Owners Association (KPOA) was formed.

Narsai David opened Kensington's first restaurant, Narsai's, at Colusa Circle.

BART started operations; a student at Kensington Elementary School was the first passenger to ride through the tunnel to San Francisco.

1973   Moeser Lane in El Cerrito was extended to Arlington Avenue, giving residents direct east-west access.

1975   The Senior Activity Center was started at the Arlington Community Church.

Kensington Park was identified by a sign.

1976   Utilities on Arlington Avenue were undergrounded through the efforts of the KIC. New street lights were installed.

Tennis courts were opened in Kensington Park.

1977   A sign board identifying the community and announcing local events was constructed by the KIC on Arlington Avenue at the south entrance to Kensington.

An intermediate age playground was built east of the Youth Hut.

1978   The KIC published the second edition of the *Survey of Kensington*.

Proposition 13, a statewide initiative, placed a limit on property taxes that could be levied. One result was a substantial decrease in revenue available to special districts.

The Kensington Symphony Orchestra was founded.

The picnic area was added to Kensington Park.

The Recreation Advisory Board, appointed by the KCSD, was dissolved.

1979   The governmental powers of the KCSD were expanded to include refuse collection.

The Tehiyah Day School, an independent Jewish school for grades K-8, had its beginning in the Youth Hut.

1980 The population of Kensington was 5,342.

A new building complex housing a hardware store, ice-cream parlor, law offices, and veterinary clinic opened on the site of the former Kensington Market.

1981 A kiosk designed for the KIC by Bart Jones was constructed in front of the Arlington Pharmacy.

1982 Incorporation was rejected by a vote of nearly two to one by Kensington residents.

The Kensington After School Educational Program (KASEP) began.

1984 The Blakemont Property Owners Association was organized to study the formation of a Geological Hazard Abatement District to abate the slide problems in the Blakemont area.

A tree view ordinance (#84-3), sponsored by the KIC, was adopted by the County Board of Supervisors.

1986 Utilities in the Colusa Circle area were undergrounded.

Kiosk at Arlington Pharmacy
Photo by Theodore Osmundson

1987 A veterinary clinic at Colusa Circle was built as Phase I of developer Ed Hammond's four-phase redevelopment program. There are currently no plans for the remaining phases.

Ordinance #87-67, which placed restrictions on residential second units, was adopted by the Board of Supervisors at the recommendation of the KIC.

The Kensington Fire Protection District (KFPD) discontinued use of volunteer firefighters.

The Youth Hut was remodeled.

1988   The permanent traffic island at Colusa Circle was constructed.

The conference room in the Youth Hut opened for adult meetings. The KIC installed lockers and window coverings.

1989   The Kensington Municipal Advisory Council (KMAC) was established by the County Board of Supervisors as a result of efforts by the KIC.

The Youth Hut was renamed the Kensington Community Center.

Kensington was annexed to the County Landscaping District. The Colusa Circle traffic island was landscaped by the KIC under the pro bono direction of landscape architect Ted Osmundson.

1990   The population of Kensington was 4,974.

1991   The KIC published *Kensington — There's an Earthquake in Your Future* and distributed it to every Kensington household.

A curbside recycling program was started in Kensington.

1992   The Kensington Roads Improvement Assessment District was established by the County Board of Supervisors (Ordinance #92-46) to resurface or rebuild all public roads over a period of three years after Kensington voters narrowly approved the project in an advisory vote.

The Kensington police dispatch service was transferred to Richmond.

The Kensington Time Capsule, to be dug up in the year 2043, was buried on the grounds of the Community Center and marked by a plaque. An Eagle Scout project, it was funded by the KIC, KPOA, and KCC.

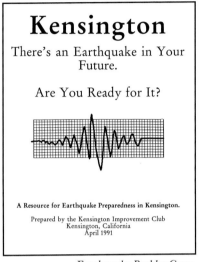

Kensington

There's an Earthquake in Your Future.

Are You Ready for It?

A Resource for Earthquake Preparedness in Kensington.

Prepared by the Kensington Improvement Club
Kensington, California
April 1991

Earthquake Booklet Cover
Design by Paul Lettieri

KENSINGTON
TIME CAPSULE
BURIED JANUARY 1, 1993
TO BE OPENED ON
JANUARY 1, 2043

Time Capsule Plaque
Photo by Paul Lettieri

1993   The name of the Kensington Community Services District was changed to the Kensington Police Protection and Community Services District in order to assure state funding to the district. (The District is still known locally as KCSD.)

1994   The KFPD Board of Directors was expanded from three to five members.

The Friends of the Kensington Library financed the extension of library hours.

1995   A contract was signed between the Kensington Fire Protection District and the El Cerrito Fire Department to provide fire protection services for Kensington. Kensington retained administrative responsibilities for the District through its elected Board of Directors.

Kensington Park Before Building Demolition, 1997
Photo by Theodore Osmundson

The KCSD Board of Directors was expanded from three to five members.

The Kensington Park Assessment District was formed to acquire eight acres of land from the West Contra Costa Unified School District for use as park land.

Kensington was designated as a Very High Fire Hazard

Kensington Park After Building Demolition, 1999
Photo by Theodore Osmundson

Severity Zone by the California Department of Forestry.

1996   The KCSD garbage collection franchise was taken over by the County Board of Supervisors, resulting in a lawsuit by the KCSD for its recovery.

1997   The KCSD recovered the franchise for garbage collection in Kensington from the County, and the lawsuit filed against the County was dropped.

A final master plan for the development of Kensington Park was completed by the Kensington Park Advisory Committee.

The Kensington Amateur Radio Operators (KARO) was organized to provide emergency communication services for Kensington in event of a disaster.

1998   The public safety building underwent seismic strengthening and was modified to comply with the requirements of the Americans with Disabilities Act. The administrative offices of the KCSD were moved downstairs.

The portable classrooms on the lower school grounds were demolished to make room for a turf field.

1999   The Kensington Public Safety building reopened following a four month renovation and remodeling of the interior.

The administrative functions of the KFPD were transferred back to Kensington from El Cerrito, and the District hired an office administrator.

The Kensington Police Department established a Reserve Police Officer Program.

Work was started on the new addition to Kensington Park.

Public Safety Building, 1999
Photo by Theodore Osmundson

Photo by Katherine Trow

Natural Setting and Land Use

1

T he town of Kensington, with a population of approximately 5,000, is an unincorporated area in the extreme southwest corner of Contra Costa County. It lies between Berkeley on the south and El Cerrito on the north and west, and shares narrow sections of its boundaries with the cities of Albany and Richmond. To the east lie Charles Lee

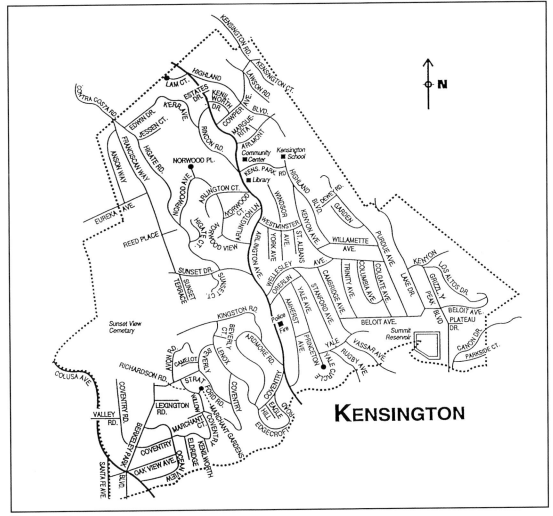

Kensington Streets

Tilden and Wildcat Canyon Regional Parks, both part of the East Bay Regional Park system.

The town, a 1.2 square mile tract of land directly opposite the Golden Gate, clings to the upper slope of the East Bay hills and peeks over the top to look down into Wildcat Canyon. Starting at the south-west corner with an elevation of 120 feet, the land slope increases sharply to a ridge at the northeast sector where Squirrel Hill rises 886 feet above sea level. One of the distinguishing features of Kensington is the steep contour of its land. From nearly every point in the community there is a dramatic, often breathtaking view of the San Francisco and San Pablo Bays and of the Golden Gate. Residents who live on the crest of the hill enjoy a panoramic view of the rolling hillsides of Tilden Park and Mt.

Early Homes in Kensington
Ardmore Path and Coventry Road, c. 1920

Diablo to the east and, on a clear day, Mt. St. Helena to the north.

Kensington's location in the Bay Area is enviable. There is easy access to Bay Area freeways and transportation systems, yet the town is isolated enough to retain a tranquil village-like atmosphere. With San Francisco just across the Bay, there is access to high quality entertainment in the form of operas, symphonies, and plays. The nearby Berkeley campus of the University of California offers lectures, concerts, and athletic events. Tilden and Wildcat Canyon Regional Parks, with their wildlands, hiking trails, and picnic areas, lie in its backyard.

NATURAL SETTING

Kensington was once a pastoral landscape of oak-speckled hills and grasslands. The Native Americans who lived in the area were hunter-gatherers and did not raise livestock or grow crops. The native plants were mostly bunch grasses and wildflowers. Constant winds from the ocean prevented many larger plants from taking hold. Relatively low, ground-hugging trees and shrubs were the only vegetation that could flourish, and they did so mostly in protected gullies and creek beds. Although most of the native plants are now gone, some creekside shrubs and trees may still be found, such as coast live oak, buckeye, and silktassel, with ferns, cow parsnip, California honeysuckle and torrey melic growing under and around them.

The effect on this natural landscape as other humans and animals began to move into the area is readily apparent in the changed landscape of today. The Spaniards introduced livestock that found the native bunch grasses delectable. Dirt ballast from the holds of their ships was loaded with dormant seeds just waiting to be blown by the wind to places where they could take hold. Other migrants brought many species of foreign plants from their homelands that were alien to the climate and soil of their

Colgate Avenue Looking North
Purdue Avenue in Background in Front of Water Tank, c. 1914
Photo by Louis L. Stein

new home. Thousands of new trees were planted, including pine and eucalyptus, which began to blot out the sunshine and prevent native plants from growing beneath their towering branches.

As development of the area began during the early 1900s, the landscape changed once again. Development was slow because of the steep slope of the land and the remoteness from transportation; however, the Kensington hills had something that would continue to draw newcomers as long as a vacant lot remained — their magnificent panoramic views. During the next 40 years nearly 2,300 homes were built, and the Kensington hills became home to more than 5,000 people. As these homes were landscaped, lawns, flowering gardens, and a rich mixture of native and hardy exotic trees and shrubs were planted. Further growth, however, is no longer an issue, since virtually all approved housing lots have been developed, and most of the few remaining lots are substandard or not buildable because of hillside slippage and steep terrain.

Panoramic View from Kensington Hills, c. 1940
Photo by Louis L. Stein

While further development may no longer be a problem for Kensington, the growth of its trees can be! Kensington residents love their trees, provided they are not too tall and obstructing their own particular view. Since nearly every part of the town boasts an unsurpassed view of the Bay and Golden Gate, these tall trees are often a source of conflict between neighbors whose once unrestricted views have become obstructed. A tree-view ordinance was proposed by the Kensington Improvement Club, and passed by the County Board of Supervisors in 1984 (Ordinance #84-3 is on file at the Kensington Library).

In spite of its growth and proximity to metropolitan areas, Kensington has managed to retain its quiet, village-like charm. Having changed little over the years, the town still represents a beautiful haven from the surrounding urban sprawl. It is often referred to as the "Shangri-La of the East Bay Hills" and well might it seem when the setting sun presents a view of crimson clouds behind Mt. Tamalpais, or on a clear night when the lights of the cities and the Bay spread out below like diamonds on black velvet.

There are many times, however, particularly in the early morning and late afternoon, when these magnificent views are veiled by swirling fog that rolls through the Golden Gate and settles over the area like a great white blanket. In spite of the fog, or maybe because of it, Kensington's climate is for the most part moderate and variable. Fog can occur any time of year; however, it is most evident in the summer months, providing a natural air conditioning. A local adage of "three days sun, three days fog" is more often true than not. But any grumbling about the summer weather pattern is usually quelled by a visit east or south.

Temperature variations are not as great as they are in most parts of California. There is, however, a definite division of the year into two seasons — one wet and one dry. Summers are dry and usually cool because of the fog and on-shore breezes. Winter is comparatively mild and often wet. Although temperatures may occasionally dip into the thirties or below, a winter freeze is rare. Rains average around 23 inches per year.

There is no square "grid-style" city street pattern in Kensington. Patterns are necessarily determined by the steep hillsides; consequently, narrow roads, twisting up and down the hills in a random pattern, are Kensington's trademark. Traffic problems and on-street parking on these narrow streets defy description.

A network of "hidden" paths criss-crosses the area between these winding streets, adding further charm to Kensington. Twelve paths have been identified

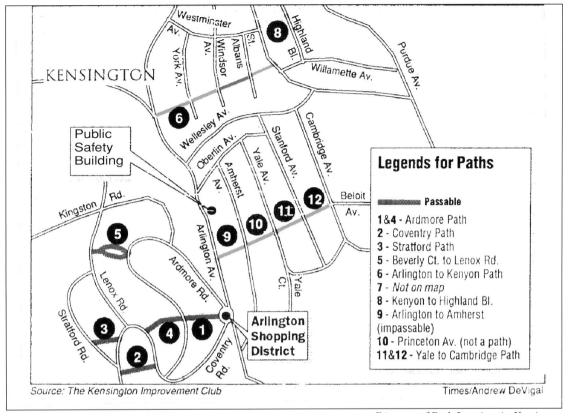

Source: The Kensington Improvement Club

Times/Andrew DeVigal

Legends for Paths

▧▧▧ **Passable**

1&4 - Ardmore Path
2 - Coventry Path
3 - Stratford Path
5 - Beverly Ct. to Lenox Rd.
6 - Arlington to Kenyon Path
7 - *Not on map*
8 - Kenyon to Highland Bl.
9 - Arlington to Amherst (impassable)
10 - Princeton Av. (not a path)
11&12 - Yale to Cambridge Path

Diagram of Path Locations in Kensington
Rosemary Barnwell

at present. Part of the mystery of these paths is their origin. Although there is no written history, this network of paths was undoubtedly established during Kensington's early development and most likely served as shortcuts between the streets. Some paths are overgrown, some are muddy and rock-strewn, while others have badly crumbling stairs. However, some do show evidence of care and maintenance by adjacent property owners. Ownership of the paths has always been in question. Although the paths were dedicated to the County on subdivision maps, the County has not accepted ownership and therefore claims no legal obligation to maintain them.

The best known and most frequented of the paths is the Stratford-Coventry-Ardmore system, used by many Kensington residents every day as a shortcut between the streets that follow the contour of the steep hillside below Arlington Avenue. Stratford Path, which leads to Coventry Road, is paved, although weedy, and not too steep. Wooden fences give the feel of a country lane. A hundred yards to the right on Coventry, just to the left of a garage with the number 636, is what appears to be a stairway to someone's property but is actually Coventry Path. It is paved and well-maintained; however, there is no identifying sign. Once up the stairs one enters a tunnel of profuse vegetation. At the top, one is once again on Coventry, which has looped around along a gentler slope. About seventy-five yards to the left, between house numbers 717 and 719, the lower part of Ardmore Path begins. It follows a fence, then bends to the right, bringing one to Ardmore Road. Across Ardmore is the wider upper half of Ardmore Path, the *Champs-Elysées* of Kensington's paths. It sports a dividing planter and is lined by regal trees. As one ascends the last of its 29 steps, the sound of traffic is heard, and one emerges into the parking lot below the Arlington shopping district.

The next longest path is the Arlington-Kenyon path, which is four blocks long. Another path, which links Yale and Cambridge Avenues via Stanford Avenue, is overgrown and all but impassable. Many of the remaining paths that aren't overgrown can look like simple driveways or entrances to houses, with nothing to suggest that they are doorways to another world.

Although there are no natural large bodies of water in Kensington, there are four main creeks. Unfortunately, there is little evidence of them today. During Kensington's developmental phase, large portions of these lovely creeks were bulldozed and/or put underground. Today, residents in these areas are paying the price for this lack of foresight by having to deal with water seepage and ground movement largely caused by underground waterways and springs.

Cerrito Creek, the only officially named creek, begins near the Summit Reservoir and proceeds underground between Vassar and Rugby Avenues, surfacing behind the Ace Hardware store at 303 Arlington Avenue, then retreating underground and running through the canyon near Edgecroft Road. The first of the other three unnamed creeks flows from the Norwood Court-Norwood Avenue area, follows Kingston Road, and continues into Sunset View Cemetery along its boundary with the East Bay Municipal Utility District Filtration Plant. The other two creeks flow along the north and south borders of the Blake Estate. Since all creeks flow through privately held land, it is unlikely that public assistance will soon be found to improve them so they can once again be enjoyed in their original state.

The Hayward Fault is the most significant geological feature in Kensington. The main trace of the fault runs through the center of town roughly parallel to

Arlington Avenue. According to the Lienkaemper fault trace map, it intersects Arlington Avenue at the Berkeley border, then runs in a northerly direction approximately 200 feet west of Arlington Avenue before splitting into a V around the Norwood Avenue/Norwood Court area. It continues through the Blake Estate, across the top of Jessen Court, and on into El Cerrito. In an ongoing study of Strawberry Creek on the nearby University of California campus, geologists recently found the long-term slippage of the fault to be 1/5 of an inch per year.

A large portion of Kensington on both sides of Arlington Avenue has been placed in the Alquist-Priolo Special Studies Zone as defined by the California division of Mines and Geology for the Hayward Fault. The fault occasionally comes to life and reminds the community of its presence by giving the land a good jolt, as it did in December of 1998 when a 4.1 magnitude earthquake centered in El Cerrito, approximately 1/2 mile from the Kensington border, shook homes and rattled dishes and nerves.

Alquist Priolo Special Studies Fault Zone (Shaded in Gray)

According to the "Regional Earthquake Probability Study" released by USGS geologists in October of 1999, there is a 70% chance that an earthquake of magnitude 6.7 or greater will occur in the Bay Area before 2030. The Study also stated that the most likely and potentially damaging quake will be centered on the Hayward Fault.

On October 21, 1868, a quake centered on the southern end of the Hayward

Fault was caused by a rupture of approximately one-half of the total fault line. It resulted in widespread damage in Hayward and San Leandro and tumbled brick buildings as far away as San Francisco. Little damage, however, was recorded north of the Oakland line.

Mystery still surrounds the history of breaks on the northern section of the Hayward Fault. Until recently, the last large quake centered in this area was thought to have occurred in 1836. In June 1997, two trenches were excavated on the grounds of El Cerrito Mira Vista golf course in an effort to search for evidence pertaining to the 1836 and other quakes. Nine-foot trenches were dug in the second fairway. Significantly, no evidence was found of the 1836 quake. Evidence did show that at least four to seven large quakes had occurred in the past 2,200 years, the most recent of which was between 1640 and 1780. A study of old mission diaries and records concludes that the 1836 quake ruptured somewhere south of San Jose.

It has been estimated that the shaking from a major Hayward Fault earthquake will be eight to twelve times stronger than that of the 1989 Loma Prieta earthquake, which damaged and destroyed buildings and freeways in San Francisco and Oakland and did major damage to the Bay Bridge. Although Loma Prieta occurred on the San Andreas fault, 75 miles away, it was felt throughout Kensington.

The other major geological feature of concern in Kensington is the unstable hillside in the Blakemont area. A major slide that includes approximately 19 acres of land extends from the top of the Blake Estate at Rincon Road through Highgate Road and Franciscan Way and into El Cerrito around Eureka Avenue. Ground movement has destroyed three homes in this area and caused both major and minor damage to many more. In 1984, residents formed the Blakemont Property Owners Association to determine if there was an economical and technically feasible way to reduce the creeping motion of the slide. The Association is currently studying the feasibility of forming a Geological Hazard Abatement District to deal with the problem.

No discussion of the natural setting of Kensington would be complete without mention of the animal kingdom that feeds upon and lives in the vegetation that grows here. Kensington has been, and still is, home to a number of wild creatures, and part of the appeal of living in Kensington is the opportunity to watch wildlife in one's own backyard. Bears and wolves were seen in the early part of the century, as well as elk that roamed the Kensington slope in search of grazing lands. These larger creatures are long gone, although from time to time an occasional sighting of an elusive mountain lion is reported. The wildlife remaining includes the very adaptable raccoons, mice, squirrels, skunks, rats, opossums, and deer — creatures who have been able to retain a semblance of their original habitats and who know how to hide.

The white-tailed deer that are prevalent in Kensington are fascinating to observe when they are not browsing on one's lettuce, prized roses, or exotic plants. Although it is said that there are a number of deerproof plants, Kensington residents have found little vegetation deer will not eat when hungry enough. Kensington's deer are sufficiently comfortable with their surroundings to wander down the middle of a street in broad daylight or dart out suddenly in front of a car from behind a roadside bush.

Raccoons will visit garbage cans for twilight treats or tap on windows for a handout. Skunks and opossums might take up residence under houses for daytime siestas. An occasional sighting of red foxes, bobcats, coyotes, or pumas might be made in the parklands bordering Kensington.

Coexisting in peace with these wild neighbors requires the ability to temper the appeal of watching wildlife in our own backyards with the ability to control their destructive tendencies.

View to Wildcat Canyon
Photo by
Paul Lettieri

LAND USE

Kensington is essentially a residential community with the majority of lots zoned R-6 for single family dwellings. Homes represent a diversity of building styles, which is one source of Kensington's character and charm. In addition to the residential sector, the town has two small commercial areas, one on Arlington Avenue and the other at Colusa Circle, both of which offer a variety of goods and services to residents within a few minutes' drive.

The largest single commercial parcel of land is the Sunset View Cemetery and

Sunset View Cemetery, c. 1930
Photo by Louis L. Stein

Mausoleum, which occupy 50.47 acres at the northwestern tip of Kensington. The land was originally part of a larger area purchased by George Baxter in 1919 from defaulted mortgages. A portion of this land was put on the market in 1920 as the "Arlington Acres" subdivision, and the remaining property was developed into the Cemetery. The Mausoleum was added in 1926 and is under separate management.

The San Pablo Filter Plant and the Summit Reservoir, owned by the East Bay Municipal Utility District, together occupy another 33.11 acres. The Filter Plant, located at 300 Berkeley Park Boulevard, is a water treatment and pumping plant used to supplement the Orinda Filter Plant. It was built in 1921 and enlarged in 1947. As a supplementary plant only, it is not in continuous use. The grounds also contain a 5.4 million gallon reservoir where treated water is stored and pumped up to Summit Reservoir for distribution.

The Summit Reservoir, located on Grizzly Peak Boulevard between Beloit Avenue and Spruce Street, was constructed in 1891, and actually predates the formation of the water district in 1923. The reservoir was originally an open body of water, but was covered and landscaped in 1972 in accordance with water quality requirements. It holds 37 million gallons of water to a maximum depth of 19.3 feet. Its overflow elevation is 816.3 feet. Emergency overflow pipes are located on the eastern side of the reservoir to direct the flow of water into the Tilden Park region should an emergency occur. Treated water is pumped to 6,700 house meters located in parts of north Berkeley and in Kensington east of Franciscan Way. (The remainder of Kensington's water is supplied by the Berryman Reservoir on Euclid Avenue in Berkeley.)

Religious and educational groups comprise the other major land owners in Kensington. The Arlington Community Church is located at 52 Arlington Avenue on property purchased from Anson Blake in 1945. The building was completed in 1948 and was remodeled and enlarged in 1950. The Unitarian Universalist Church of Berkeley, at 1 Lawson Road, occupies a spectacular setting on top of Squirrel Hill and commands a sweeping view of the entire Bay Area. The building was constructed in 1961 on 5.94 acres of land donated by the renowned architect Bernard Maybeck.

The West Contra Costa Unified School District owns the land on which the Kensington Elementary School and playgrounds are located. The District transferred title for a portion of its land to the Kensington Community Services District for construction of the Youth Hut (Kensington Community Center) in 1955, and for the Kensington Library, which was completed in 1965. A smaller piece of property was donated to supplement Arlington Church property for use as a parking lot opposite the library. The remaining eight acres of unused school property were purchased by the Kensington Community Services District, through a bond issue in 1995, to be used for park and recreation facilities. A smaller portion of land dedicated to municipal use is the public safety building at 217 Arlington Avenue which houses the Kensington fire and police departments.

Hidden in a 10.5-acre tract of land at 70 Rincon Road just off the Arlington lies one of the finest homes and gardens in the Bay Area, the magnificent Blake Estate owned by the University of California. The estate was deeded to the University by Anson Stiles Blake and his wife, Anita Symmes Blake, and is now used as the official residence of the President of the University.

Blake Garden
Photo by Theodore Osmundson

Blake Garden Reflecting Pool
Photo by Theodore Osmundson

When the Blakes first acquired the land in the early 1900s, the site on the Kensington hillside was bare of vegetation except for scrub brush, grass, and a few native shrubs and trees. Knowing his wife was an avid horticulturist, Anson situated the house carefully so it would serve as a windbreak for the extensive gardens planned for the property. Anita's sister, Mabel Symmes, a landscape architect and UC Berkeley graduate, laid out plans for the garden. The Blakes brought many exotic plants from their home in Berkeley, and Anita added hundreds of unusual varieties which she brought home from her frequent travels throughout the world. Over the years, more than 2,500 species were transplanted to the Blake Gardens, creating a collector's paradise. With the temperate Mediterranean climate that prevailed, most thrived. It is said today that the gardens have a greater variety of plants than Golden Gate Park.

The five distinct garden areas originally designed by Mabel Symmes are still maintained today. A formal garden lies at the front of the house, complemented by a beautiful reflecting pool bordered by graceful magnolia trees and lush hydrangeas. To the north is a large redwood grove, planted by the Blakes. On the west side of the house is a drought-tolerant garden where the graded terraces are defined by formal diamond-shaped beds filled with cistus, correa, euphorbia, rosemary, and artemisia. A fourth area, called the cottage garden, is for cut flowers and vegetables. This colorful corner is where roses, flowering annuals, and perennials are grown to provide floral arrangements for the home. A large outcropping of blue-gray lawsonite, a rare volcanic rock, marks the way to the final section of the gardens — the "Australian Hollow," an area filled with plants native to Australia. The estate is bordered by two streams. A covey of quail, who have made the area their home, adds to the charm.

The semi-public gardens are used for teaching programs by the University's Department of Landscape Architecture, UC Davis, UC Extension, Diablo Valley College, and Merritt College. Students often assist the four full-time staff members in maintaining the garden through work-study programs. The impressive grounds are open to the public on most weekdays with the exception of university holidays. They are closed to the public on weekends.

In 1948, three acres of the garden and a second house on the Blake property, the "pink mansion," which had belonged to Anson's brother, Edwin, were sold to Noel Sullivan for use as a Carmelite Monastery. The property was sealed off from the rest of the world by a 12 foot high wall on all sides to become the lifelong residence of the only order of cloistered nuns in the Catholic diocese of Oakland. A long driveway leads to a chapel and small anteroom. A sign hangs above the buzzer to the anteroom: "Please enter and ring bell inside." Upon entering, one sees a revolving wooden screen in the center of a wall in front of which is a table with a pad and pencil. All communication takes place behind the screen. One nun known as an extern, however, can come and go from the convent to buy groceries and conduct necessary business in the outside world.

The nuns, who have chosen to isolate themselves from the world and spend their days in prayer and meditation, are members of an order founded in Syria in 1160. The Kensington monastery is one of nine such monasteries in California. The 1987 official register with vital information about all religious communities in the diocese states only that the monastery houses seven professed unshod Carmelites under solemn vows of poverty.

Behind the locked doors and high walls lies a world no outsider can penetrate. All that is known is that the order is a contemplative, self-governing body whose members have taken a vow of poverty and silence. Beyond that, the "pink mansion" is a silent reminder of the cloistered monastic life of the Middle Ages.

Carmelite Monastery, 1999
Photo by Natalie Salsig

SOURCES

Barnwell, Rosemary, Kensington Improvement Club study of "Kensington Paths."

Blakemont Property Owners Association newsletter, 6/97.

Danielson, Charli, Native Here Nursery.

District Office, East Bay Municipal Utility District.

"From Fellowship House to Community Church," 1982.

Geomatrix Consultants, Inc., "Report to Kensington Fire District," 10/97.

Harza report to Kensington Fire District, 6/6/97.

Kensington Improvement Club. *There's an Earthquake in Your Future.* April 1991.

Lienkaemper Mapping Service, 1992 report.

Norcross, John, Blake Garden Master Gardener.

Sanders, Robert, "Taking Measure of the Hayward Fault," *Berkeley Magazine*, University of California, Spring, 1998.

San Francisco Chronicle, 4/22/98; 10/15/99.

West County Times: 9/14/87; 2/6/88; 12/18/90; 10/15/99.

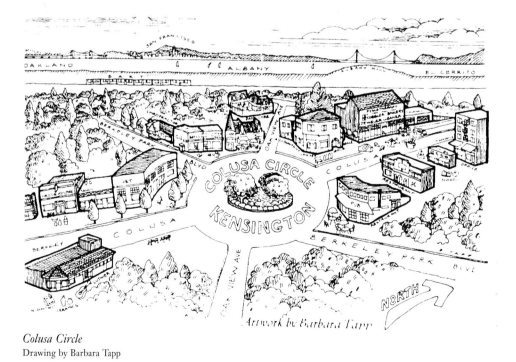

Colusa Circle
Drawing by Barbara Tapp

HISTORY AND DEVELOPMENT

2

The early historical evolution of the Kensington area can be divided into three periods: Indian settlements, Spanish expeditions, and the Mexican period. The earliest archaeological dates gleaned from the large mounds of shells accumulated at many spots along the Bay shore indicate an Indian presence at least as early as 2000 B.C., but an area of such rich food resources may have been occupied much earlier.

The Indians apparently came in two waves: first a Hokan-speaking people, followed by Penutian-speaking tribes around 300 to 500 A.D. who had mixed with or displaced the Hokans by the time of the Spanish arrival. The Huchiuns were the predominant tribe in the Kensington area. (The Spanish also used other phonetic spellings: Juchiyunes, Jutchiunes, Chuchillones, Xuiyuns.) They occupied a large portion of the eastern shore of San Francisco Bay, extending from Temescal Creek in the North Oakland area at least to the lower San Pablo and Wildcat Creek drainages in the present area of Richmond.

The Spaniards referred to all Indian tribes living in the Bay Area, including a region stretching to a bit south of Carmel and Salinas, as Costanoans ("people of the coast"), and the Huchiuns apparently spoke a sub-group of the Costanoan language called Chochenyo. Costanoan is thought to be a member of the family of languages called Penutian. Descendants of the Bay Area Indians, however, disliked the Spanish name Costanoan and preferred to be called Ohlones. Recently a group of about 200 biological descendants of all the Costanoan linguistic groups requested governmental recognition as the Ohlone tribe.

The Bay Area Indians lived in a number of politically independent villages located near the many

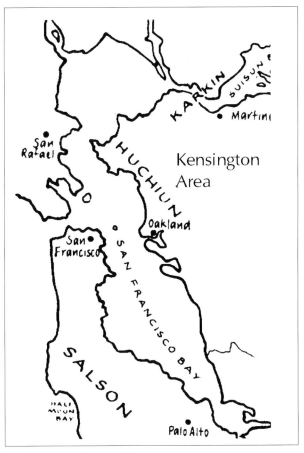

Early Indian Tribe Areas
Randall Milliken

creeks and sloughs flowing into San Francisco Bay. Each tribe had its own territory and chief. They dwelt in peace with their neighbors and in harmony with the natural environment, living on a wide variety of fish, fowl, small game, and plants supplied by the marshlands, bay, and hillsides. Their two primary sources of food were shellfish and acorns, which required specialized processing to leach out the tannic acid.

In 1769, the King of Spain extended the Spanish empire north of Mexico into California territory, and in 1770 the Spaniards established a town and mission on Monterey Bay. In March of 1772, the Lieutenant Pedro Fages expedition came from Monterey through the Santa Clara Valley into the East Bay (see map on page 12). At the time, according to anthropologist Randall Milliken (1995), "The political landscape of the San Francisco Bay region was a mosaic of tiny tribal territories, each some eight to twelve miles in diameter, each containing a population of some two hundred to four hundred individuals." The expedition was greeted "with great joy" by the Huchiuns. A member of the party, Father Juan Crespi, noted: "We found a good village of heathen very fair and bearded, who did not know what to do, they were so happy to see us in their village. They gave us many cacomites, amoles (the root of a plant used for soap), and two dead geese, dried and stuffed with grass. . ." (pp. 36-51). The expedition passed through the Kensington area from what is now El Cerrito to Wildcat Canyon on a series of mapping expeditions and to search for settlement sites. On the way they gave names to many of the current landmarks such as "El Cerrito" (the little hill), later renamed Albany Hill, and "Cerrito Creek," from which El Cerrito was named. After 1776 the Spanish crown occupied the Bay Area to strengthen the northern flank of the empire. The area around Kensington, however, was used by the padres at Mission Dolores solely for grazing cattle and horses.

As colonization of their land took place, the number of Indian tribes in the area was heavily reduced by epidemics of newly introduced diseases. In addition, many Indians left their villages and moved to the missions, believing such a move was the only reasonable alternative in a transformed world. Milliken states, "By the year 1810 the tribal territories in all but the most northerly reaches of the San Francisco Bay region were empty" (pp. 36-51). But a century later, exciting evidence of the Indian occupation in this area was discovered as homes were built on the Kensington hillsides. Long-time Kensington resident Mary Lee Cole, whose family built one of the first homes in Kensington on Amherst Avenue (circa

1920), is quoted in the Kensington Business and Services Directory: "When we dug for a patio, we unearthed layer after layer of arrowheads, sea shells and bones we could only wonder about." Early residents who built homes in the vicinity of Squirrel Hill remember their children bringing home arrowheads they had uncovered while building forts and sliding down the grassy hillside on cardboard boxes.

In 1821 the Mexican Republic replaced the Spanish monarchy. The national government generously distributed land in California to its soldiers in order to establish cattle ranchos and to further economic development of the territory. In recognition of his 13 years of military service, first to Spain and then to Mexico, Francisco María Castro (born 1775 in Sinaloa, Mexico) was granted Rancho San Pablo in 1823. The grant included most of what is now Kensington, El Cerrito, Richmond, and San Pablo, and was part of the diocese of Mission Dolores in San Francisco.

After his retirement from the Mexican army in 1826, Francisco Castro and his wife, Gabriela Berryessa, built a home in the Alvarado Creek area of his newly acquired land. In 1829 the home was destroyed by fire, and a second structure was built in the same area. Members of the Castro family lived on the Rancho until long after gold was discovered in California.

On Francisco's death in 1831, the land was partitioned among his wife and 11 children. The southern portion, including Kensington, was given to his youngest son, Victor. Victor Castro was born in 1820 and was married to Luisa Martínez in 1837. He and his wife employed 200 Indians to build their home in 1839, a beautiful two-story adobe hacienda that stood on the present site of El Cerrito Plaza. The hacienda was the first dwelling to be constructed in the area. It soon became a gathering place for many notables, including Bret Harte, who was a constant visitor. It remained a landmark until 1956, when it burned to the ground. A plaque commemorates its location, and one of its bricks was saved and incorporated into one of the original Plaza buildings.

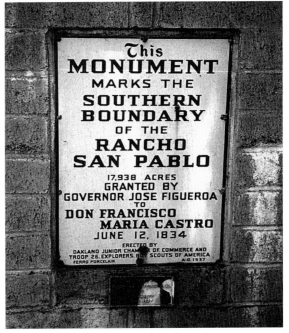

Plaque Near El Cerrito Plaza in Front of Wells Fargo Bank on San Pablo Avenue
Photo by Paul Lettieri

Victor Castro developed his land, raising grain, fruits, vegetables, and livestock. Indian men worked his cattle on the hillsides of what one day would become Kensington, and Indian women on the Rancho kept the house and did the cooking under the supervision of Castro's wife, Luisa. Recognizing the need for a convenient means of transportation across the Bay, Castro built a wharf on Point Isabel (named for his daughter) from which supplies and food, as well as passengers, could be ferried around the Bay and to and from the growing community of Yerba Buena (San Francisco). He also built a corral, a slaughterhouse, and a hotel on the point.

The American takeover of California in 1848 and the gold rush days of 1849 brought about drastic changes as hordes of gold-seekers swarmed into the Bay Area. American settlers began to homestead land in the East Bay, and the region quickly changed character. In 1850, California entered the American Union as the thirty-first state, and Contra Costa County was formed by an act of the State Legislature as one of the original 27 counties. The El Cerrito-Kensington region became part of San Pablo township. On June 14, 1852, Victor Castro was elected as one of five men to serve on the first Contra Costa County Board of Supervisors. A crude network of county roads was established. Most were ungraded, rutted, and generally in poor condition — muddy in the winter and dusty in the summer. However, they provided a thoroughfare for horse-drawn wagons used by farmers to carry their goods to local markets. Arlington Avenue was known as Road #6 and led to El Sobrante Rancho and the interior.

During this period, a number of settlers began to buy portions of Rancho San Pablo from Victor Castro, who was disposing of large tracts of his land to pay off taxes and other debts. Since the land had never been surveyed, many parcels were sold without clearing title. Squatters were also claiming land, and the actions of unscrupulous speculators and conflicting interests of buyers led to prolonged lawsuits. The vast holdings of the family began to dwindle as Castro became a victim of his inability to manage his own property, and the family soon found itself living in a state of landed poverty. By 1896, when a court decision had finally been reached on holdings of the original land grant, Castro had lost most of his land to new settlers and lawyers or had sold it for insignificant amounts. By the time of his death in 1900, he retained little more than his adobe and a few surrounding acres.

As a result of the court decision approving the final settlement of land claims against Castro, more than 600 acres, representing about two-thirds of present-day Kensington, were placed in Lot #1 and awarded to George Leviston, a San Francisco attorney who was forced to accept land in lieu of fees earned during the long litigation process. Other portions of Kensington were placed in Lot #2, awarded to Philip Galpin, and in Lots #3 and #3 ½, awarded to Richard O'Neil, a trustee for the Castros.

EARLY SUBDIVISIONS

The incredibly tangled title to the Castro land holdings and resulting litigation discouraged prospective farmers and merchants from establishing substantial enterprises in the Kensington area before 1896. However, in 1890, Anson Blake and Berkeley realtor George Schmidt had begun to subdivide large farm tracts and to sell off smaller residential lots. Anson Blake himself bought a portion of Rancho San Pablo in 1892, much of which lay in the Kensington area.

By this time a few merchants had begun to establish business enterprises near Castro's adobe. However, between 1900 and 1925 Kensington was still a largely undeveloped grassy hillside covered with dairy farms and adjoining pasture land. Jack rabbits, deer, and coyotes abounded in the area, and children climbed the haystacks and chased the cattle.

Among the prominent dairies in the Kensington and upper El Cerrito area were the Home Dairy of William Hinds, John Balra's Sunset Dairy, John Merlo's Stege Dairy, Allois Andregg's Dairy, and the Poppy Hill Creamery. Milk deliveries were made by wagon and later by trucks to local homes and retail markets in Berkeley and Oakland. The only other development on the hillsides near Kensington was a saw mill and dry kiln built in 1896 near the present site of the Summit Reservoir. The blue gum eucalyptus logs proved unsuitable for building, and the mill was shut down.

Primary residential development began in the early 1900s, and the first survey of the Kensington area was made in 1911. Two of the original surveyors were from England. One, by the name of Robert Bousefield, named the land "Kensington" after South Kensington, the London borough in which he lived.

In 1901, George Shima, originally Kinji Ushijima, known as the "Japanese potato king" because he held thousands of acres of rich potato land in the delta region, bought ten acres of land along Cerrito Creek from Arlington Avenue east

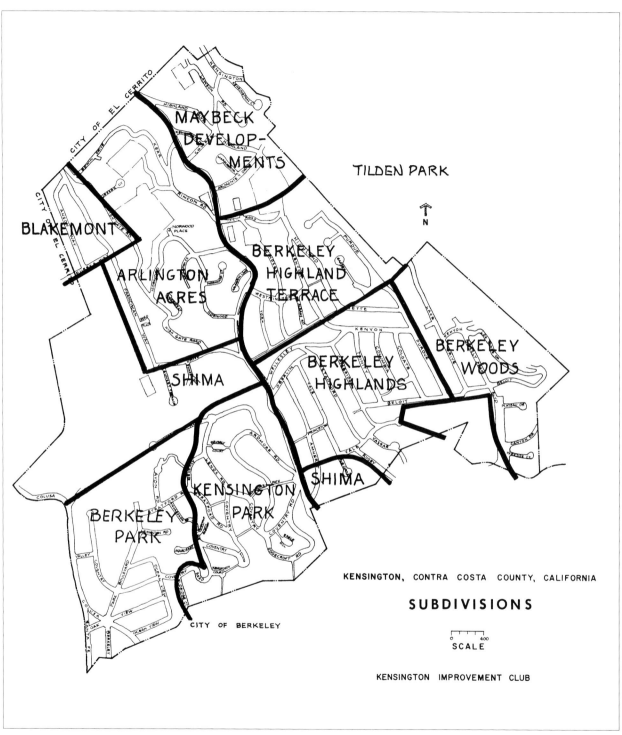

Original Subdivisions

to Rugby. The parcel of hillside land, which lay east of Arlington Avenue and just north of the county line, was intended to be his home. He fenced it in and planted a number of acacia trees, many of which are still standing on Rugby, Yale, and Amherst Avenues. Each year he staged a community picnic on his Kensington property. Shima, however, never built his home. He later sold all his property, except for the one-acre triangular lot between Amherst and Arlington, to J. W. Beazier, who developed Yale Circle and adjacent areas.

Ironically, Kensington owes its initial growth in population not only to visionary real estate developers, but also to two major disasters, the San Francisco earthquake and fire of 1906, and later, the Berkeley fire of 1923. The earthquake prompted displaced residents to look to the East Bay for housing; however, buyers still came slowly to the remote area of Kensington. A few wealthy persons came by auto, others on horseback or by horse and buggy.

In 1910 Lot #1, the property awarded to George Leviston by the court following litigation on Victor Castro's land, was sold to speculators. The largest individual piece was resold to Frank J. Woodward and Associates, who planned its future subdivision. Woodward borrowed money on the southerly 72 acres from George P. Baxter, and on the northerly 45 acres from Mrs. Harriet

The "Caudron House" at 264 Arlington
Viewed from Amherst Avenue Looking West, c. 1920

Arlington and Amherst Gateway Looking North, c. 1915
Photo by Louis L. Stein

Waters Blake, mother of Anson Blake. Woodward later defaulted on both notes.

Land development companies were now beginning to acquire subdivisions for development, and by 1911 several companies owned most of Kensington. However, few homes were being constructed. Lots in the Berkeley Park subdivision (bounded roughly by Kingston Road on the north, Colusa Avenue on the west, Cerrito Creek and Visalia Avenue on the south, and a line halfway between Arlington and Colusa Avenues on the east) were put on the market in 1911 by Eugene L. Brock of the Berkeley Investment Company. That same year the Dodge, Ver Mehr Company began to advertise lots for sale in the Kensington Park subdivision, west of Arlington Avenue at Ardmore and Coventry, featuring "The Residential Tract That Will Make Berkeley Famous." That slogan, combined with the unsurpassed view of San Francisco Bay and the Golden Gate that the Kensington hillside offered, began to attract buyers.

About the same time, Meikle, Brock, and Skidmore of the Berkeley Investment Company constructed an ornate arched gateway over Amherst at the corner of Arlington. The gateway served as an entrance to the future development of their Berkeley Highlands subdivision, which encompassed most of the land bounded by what is now Arlington, Wellesley, Willamette, and Purdue Avenues, and Cerrito Creek. For immediate access to the development, Brock negotiated a right of way over Shima's property, and Amherst Avenue was graded as an entrance. In 1912 the company also constructed the first commercial building in Kensington at 264 Arlington Avenue — the Caudron House (later known as Fellowship House and still later as the Roth Building) — for use as a land sales office and residence.

BERKELEY HIGHLANDS TERRACE BRANCH OFFICE, AT WESTMINSTER AND ARLINGTON.
(Telephone AShberry 1441).

Real Estate Office for Berkeley Highlands Terrace, c. 1937
Photo by Louis L. Stein

The real estate office occupied the space where the beauty parlor is now located, and a restaurant was placed in the northern section of the building, where realtors served prospective clients a free lunch before showing them property. The building remains a landmark today; the gateway, however, was removed in 1938.

In 1912 the Oakland Traction Company agreed to extend its street car line up Arlington Avenue to Kensington, and tracks were laid by the developer at a cost of $33,000. The "Kensington Park" terminus of streetcar #7 was located in front of the Caudron House.

Amherst Avenue Looking South, c. 1912
(Photo Taken from Wellesley Avenue)
Photo by Louis L. Stein

Meikle, Brock, and Skidmore opened their Berkeley Highlands subdivision in 1913. Access to Kensington by street car had now made this and all subdivisions more accessible.

In 1914, lots in Berkeley Highland Terrace were offered for sale by the F. R. Peake Company, and Kensington boasted a total of ten homes. Some of the first homes were built on Amherst, Ardmore, and Coventry Avenues. At that point, further subdividing was put on hold until the end of World War I.

El Cerrito was incorporated as a city in 1917. The incorporation movement triggered an intense fight, pitting El Cerrito residents against the Kensington farmers and dairymen who had occupied the hills for years and had no desire to pay city taxes on their farm property to finance facilities and improvements they would rarely use. They also feared city development would eventually scuttle their hillside operations.

When the proposal for incorporation was first received by the County Board of Supervisors in Martinez, the Supervisors readily admitted they knew very little about the area

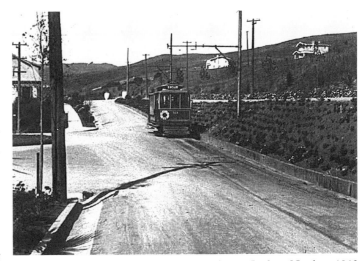

Arlington Avenue Looking North, c. 1912
Fellowship House at Left, Amherst Avenue Homes at Upper Right
Current Bus Stop and Parking Area at Left Foreground
Photo by Louis L. Stein

and in fact were not even sure of its location. In due time, all five Supervisors visited El Cerrito and were lavishly feted by the incorporation proponents. The fight with the dairymen was finally resolved in a compromise plan whereby the Supervisors drew the boundaries of the proposed city of El Cerrito to exclude areas where there was strong opposition — Kensington, Berkeley Park, and what is now Sunset View Cemetery.

In 1919 Frank Woodward defaulted on the loans made to him by George Baxter and Harriet Waters Blake to acquire George Leviston's Lot #1 (the property awarded to him following litigation of Victor Castro's land), and Woodward was forced to surrender possession of the land to Baxter and Blake. Baxter put a portion of his land on the market as "Arlington Acres," the first subdivision to open after the war. The remaining property was developed into Sunset View Cemetery. Still, few houses were being constructed, and in 1920 Kensington's population was only 226. Nevertheless, developers continued to open up the area with the subdivisions of Berkeley Woods, the Blakemont tract, and the property owned by architect Bernard Maybeck.

Thus was Kensington born — evolved from the seeds of protest, its boundaries set by exclusion rather than inclusion — destined to be a leftover pocket of unincorporated land under the jurisdiction of the county. It is interesting to note that the legacy of independence and self-determination shown by Kensington's early dairymen continues to manifest itself today as residents have rejected, on four different occasions, all attempts to change their governmental status.

Rare Snowstorm, Arlington Avenue and Wellesley Looking North, c. 1931
Photo by Louis L. Stein

Rare Snowstorm, Arlington Avenue and Amherst Looking North, c. 1931
Photo by Louis L. Stein

A COMMUNITY EVOLVES

In 1921 the Kensington Improvement Club was started, and the new community began to organize itself. The first meeting was held at the home of William Farley on Ardmore Road. Forty-eight registered voters attended. The same year the first deputy sheriffs, Howard, Kleeburger, and Woolsey, were hired to protect residents from hunters.

In 1922, Mrs. Harriet Waters Blake and the families of two of her sons, Anson and Edwin, were forced to move from their homes on Piedmont Avenue in Berkeley when the University pre-empted their land to build Memorial Stadium. To provide new homes, Mrs. Blake divided the Kensington property, which she had previously acquired through default on the Woodward note, among her four children. The Blake families on Piedmont Avenue moved to Kensington and began to develop their properties into what became known as the Blake Estate. The Anson Blake family built a Mediterranean-style house designed by architect Walter Bliss. On the adjoining land the Edwin Blake family built the "pink mansion," which included a wing for the elder Mrs. Blake. The Blakes did not refer to their property as the Blake Estate. To them it was known as "Adelante," a Spanish word meaning "further out and higher up." Looking at photographs of the construction of the house in 1922, it is easy to understand why they chose the name. The estate, now known throughout the area for its distinctive beauty, has become a magnet for tourists and visitors.

On his death in 1948, Edwin Blake's share of the property, including the "pink mansion," was sold to Noel Sullivan for use as a Carmelite monastery. In 1957 the Anson Blakes willed their 10.5-acre estate to their alma mater, the University of California, with the right to occupy the property for life. Following the death of Mrs. Blake in 1962, the house and gardens became available for University purposes. The house was remodeled in 1969 to become the official residence of the President of the University of California, and the gardens became a working laboratory for students in the University of California Department of Landscape Architecture. (For more information on the Blake Estate, see the chapter on "Natural Setting.")

The foundations for Kensington's utility services were laid gradually throughout this developmental period. The Stege Sanitary District was formed in 1913 to provide sanitary services to Kensington, El Cerrito, and Richmond Annex, marking the first unification in the area. In the early days, water was often obtained from artesian wells and open creeks. Later, piped water was supplied by the People's Water Company, which merged into the East Bay Water Company in 1916, and which was later absorbed into

Edgecroft Road and Coventry, with Fellowship House in Background, to the Right of Car, c. 1912
Photo by Louis L. Stein

the East Bay Municipal Utility District in 1923. Electrical and gas lines were brought in by PG&E in 1922, and the first street lights were installed, largely through the efforts of Anson Blake and his partner Lee Howard. Telephone service was installed by the Pacific Telephone and Telegraph Company in the late 1920s.

The second major catastrophe that became a catalyst for Kensington's rapid expansion occurred on September 17, 1923. Sparks from a small brush fire in Wildcat Canyon crossed Grizzly Peak Boulevard near Marin Avenue in Berkeley, igniting the roof of a wood shingled house. Within a few hours, the fire had spread and engulfed virtually all the area in Berkeley north of the University campus. Firemen from as far away as San Francisco stood by helplessly as the narrow water mains of the East Bay Water Company (predecessor to EBMUD) prevented an adequate water supply from reaching hydrants. In all, 584 homes were destroyed within two hours, and many more were damaged. Nine out of ten University of California professors lost their homes.

As a result of the fire, many displaced homeowners relocated to nearby Kensington, and the need for schools and services became more pressing. In 1925 an elementary school was established in Kensington consisting of two portable buildings moved from Richmond, and the first Kensington PTA was formed. Five children were registered in kindergarten. In 1927 the first Boy Scout Troop was organized and sponsored by the Improvement Club.

During this period, George Friend, a former vaudeville actor, began to sell homes in the fashionable Thousand Oaks neighborhood in Berkeley which was being developed by his father-in-law, John Spring. Friend ran a thriving office near the top of Solano Avenue (later Ortman's Ice Cream Parlor, now Starbucks). In 1926 he turned his attention to Kensington and opened one of the last subdivisions, the exclusive "Arlington Estates," where homes were advertised as costing "not less that $5,000" and offering "beautiful villa sites commanding a marvelous marine panorama."

ARCHITECTURALLY AND HISTORICALLY NOTEWORTHY BUILDINGS IN KENSINGTON

The Anson Blake House, built in 1922-24, is the grandest of all the buildings in Kensington. Author Mark Wilson (1979) calls it an "opulent, Italian Renaissance-style villa," and the "two-story, stuccoed facade, with its Renaissance loggia on the north wing and restrained neo-Classic detailing on the second floor," impressive (p. 139). Inside the mansion is a collection of antique furniture, including a giant four-poster bed used by President William Taft. Hanging on the walls is a collection of prized paintings.

In 1967, when it was decided that UC presidents would occupy the house, it was in a dilapidated condition. It was remodeled in 1969 under the direction of Mrs. Geraldine Knight Scott working with architect Ronald Brocchini. New parking lots, outdoor lighting, retaining walls, and steps were added. Charles J. Hitch was the first president to occupy the house in 1969.

The building located at 264 Arlington Avenue, first known as the Caudron House (after the Caudron family who owned the house in the early 1920s) and later as Fellowship House, also occupies a unique place in the history of Kensington because so many community organizations and programs had their beginning within its walls. As mentioned earlier, it is the oldest commercial building in Kensington, having been constructed in 1912 by Meikle, Brock, and Skidmore as a land sales office and residence. It

The Anson Blake House
Photo by Theodore Osmundson

was designed in the Dutch Colonial Revival style, with a gambrel roof and a porte cochère (carriage entrance).

In 1932, Fellowship House was rented for $50 a month by the Bay Association of Congregational Churches to be used as a church and Sunday School. However, since it was the only building in Kensington suitable for a meeting place, the church agreed the building could serve as a community center as well. John Gregg was the first director, and Anson Blake was appointed a member of the first Directing Committee.

In 1942 the building was put up for sale. Fellowship House then went through a series of owners before being bought by Stanley Roth in 1963, and for the next thirty-odd years it was called the Roth Building. It became headquarters for the Kensington Police Department in 1946 and continued until 1970 when the new public safety building was built at 217 Arlington Avenue. Stan Roth used the space vacated by the Police Department for his real estate and lumber brokerage businesses. In 1996 the building was sold to Eugene Millstein, who moved his real estate office to the building. Millstein replaced the crumbling foundation and renovated the interior.

Kensington is the home of many architecturally noteworthy buildings. Many of the Bay Area's important architects designed houses in Kensington, and some designed and built homes for themselves and their families here. W. R. Yelland, who designed the whimsical buildings in the Neighborhood Center (discussed later in this chapter), lived a few doors away from a delightful half-timbered house on Lenox Road which he designed in the Hansel and Gretel style in 1928. John Hudson Thomas' residence on Norwood Avenue, built in 1930, is multi-gabled in the neo-Tudor style with more Period Revival flavor than most of his work. Another well-known architect who worked in this area, Paul Hammarberg, also designed and built his home on Norwood Avenue. Roger Lee designed a complex of three houses on Reed Place in the 1950s. Lee was another important Bay Area architect who lived in Kensington — on Highgate Road just east of these houses.

"Hansel and Gretel" House on Lenox Road
Photo by Paul Lettieri

The internationally renowned architect Bernard Maybeck, who owned a number of parcels of land in Kensington, built a house on Purdue for his son and daughter-in-law, Wallen and Jacomena Maybeck. The 1937 house is described in Kenneth Cardwell's book on Maybeck (1983): "Its isolated position above dry grass hills beyond the area of city fire protection was one of the factors that led Maybeck to his final demonstration of fireproof building. . . . The Wallen Maybeck house boldly employed concrete and corrugated iron roofing to create a fire-proof structure of unique character" (pp. 232-3).

Another house of architectural interest is the 1928 Novitzky house on Sunset Drive.

This gambrel-roofed house combines elements of Craftsman architecture with features of a log cabin. Dr. Josef Novitzky, owner, designer, and builder, blended new and previously used materials in the construction. Eucalyptus logs from the East Bay hills can be found on the interior walls. Cobblestones from San Francisco streets separate the stucco and wood areas on the exterior, and timbers salvaged from a soap factory in Berkeley support the two-story living room.

Two other buildings, on opposite ends of a spectrum of stateliness, are worth mentioning. The Sunset View Mausoleum on the grounds of Sunset View Cemetery is, according to Mark Wilson, "a fine, Renaissance-style building built in 1927 with marble brought from Europe" (p. 140). The other is a small shack in the canyon off Sunset Drive where a group of Portola Junior High School students from Kensington and El Cerrito formed a rock band and began rehearsals in the 1960s. The band became the Creedence Clearwater Revival, which achieved international recognition before it disbanded in 1972.

KENSINGTON'S COMMERCIAL DEVELOPMENT

In 1928 it was discovered that, because of the grading done for Amherst Avenue in 1911 to open up the Berkeley Highlands subdivision, the lots still owned by George Shima in the gore (triangle) between Arlington and Amherst Avenues had been left with no deed restrictions placed on them. This discovery made it possible for Shima to sell the one acre of land to Raymond Price, who began construction of a series of buildings that were to become the commercial hub of upper Kensington. The corner building at 299 Arlington Avenue was designed by Berkeley architect E. L. Snyder. It housed Louis Stein's Arlington Pharmacy, a classic country-style drugstore replete with an old fashioned five-stool soda fountain, a circulating library where local residents could borrow books for ten cents apiece, and a post office.

The Pharmacy soon became the local headquarters for neighborhood news and a favorite destination for passengers on the Arlington Avenue #7 streetcar, which ran up the west side of Arlington and terminated across the street. Patrons at the soda fountain could watch the conductor disconnect the cable at one end of the car and reattach it at the other to reverse its direction for the return run to Berkeley. Sometimes neighborhood children joined in the fun, helping the conductor reverse the direction of the seats. The closing of the street car line in June of 1948, when it was replaced by bus service, was a sad occasion as recalled by Louis Stein: "On the day when the last street

Arlington Pharmacy and Shops, c. 1956
Photo by Louis L. Stein

Arlington Pharmacy Interior Fountain Looking North, c. 1950
Photo by Louis L. Stein

car came through we all sat around in the drugstore and had coffee and talked until almost one in the morning." To them it was more than just the loss of a beloved street car — it signaled the end of an era. The Pharmacy was operated by Louis Stein from 1928 until his retirement in 1956 and remains a landmark in the Arlington Avenue commercial area today. Although the original post office from the 1930s was removed in the early 1940s, postal services were reestablished in 1959 when the Pharmacy was appointed a "contracting station" with limited services available. Through this arrangement, the Postal Service leases space in the building, and in return, the employees of the Pharmacy run the post office.

Across the street at 304 Arlington, the current site of the Chevron Station, a group of "fanciful" buildings was designed and built in 1927 by the young architect W. R. Yelland, who lived around the corner on Coventry Road. The Yelland complex of three buildings, later known as the Neighborhood Center, was developed during the same period as his best known work, Thornburg Village (now called Normandy Village), on Spruce Street near the UC Berkeley campus. Both projects shared the stylistic vocabulary of the medieval rural French architecture that Yelland first encountered during his wartime posting in Normandy. Yelland's rendition of the style emphasized its playful, fairy-tale character, quite evident in the few surviving photographs of the Kensington buildings.

The Neighborhood Center included Kensington's first fire station, which housed its volunteer fire department, and two smaller detached buildings. One was a gas station operated by Fred Wallis, who also served as Kensington's first fire chief, and the other contained three storefronts. Tenants included Hertneck's Grocery and Roy Sulligar's real estate office. Louis Stein remembered Sulligar as a "funny old guy, a little retired mining engineer who was sloppy as hell and who walked around in knickers" (*North News*). Mr. Sulligar lived in one of Kensington's first homes on Coventry Road.

A local writer, Eugene Neuhaus, on reviewing Yelland's building on Shattuck Avenue (occupied at that time by Tupper and Reed Music Store), quoted his young son's reaction to the building: "Wouldn't downtown be interesting if all the stores were like that?" The boy's comment might equally have applied to the storybook facade of the Kensington project. The quaint, picturesque shops, despite their proximity to the fire station, burned down in the early 1950s. The fire house, however, was spared. The Center stores were not rebuilt, and the land was later purchased by Standard Oil to enlarge its station.

The 1930s saw the rapid growth of this commercial nucleus. Stein's Pharmacy was soon joined by an expansion of small shops to the north, including a grocery store, barber shop, and dry cleaners. *Kelts' Geographical Directory* for 1936 lists the Arlington Beauty Shop owned by Guy and Evelyn Wood at 287 Arlington, the Arlington Shoe Repair (later the first Young's Market) at 291 Arlington, the Arlington Cleaners at 293 Arlington, the

Original Standard Oil Station, c. 1950
Photo by Louis L. Stein

Kensington Standard Oil Station, 1966
Photo by Louis L. Stein

Chevron Station, 1973
Photo by Louis L. Stein

Arlington Variety and Arlington Electric, c. 1975
Now Arlington Wines and Inn Kensington
Photo by Louis L. Stein

Arlington Grocery at 295 Arlington, and the Arlington Meat and Vegetable Market at 297 Arlington. Over the years, various occupants of these shops came and went, including Bob and Alice Greenwood's Arlington Electric and Radio Shop and the popular Arlington Variety Store, where children congregated after school to buy penny candies.

Aside from the Pharmacy, the only original business in the Arlington shopping district that remains today is Young's Market. In 1938 Leon Young moved his store from its original site at 291 Arlington Avenue to a new building that he constructed a few doors to the north. A more genuine family-run market could hardly be found, and this is part of the secret of its remarkable longevity. Leon and his family were Kensington residents, and all six of his children worked in the market at various times. Sons Ben and Ralph took over the management of the market in the mid-60s and in 1978 took full ownership. Two years later Ralph's partnership was bought out by Steve Gaustad, a long-time employee. For many years Ben's four children, as well as several members of Steve's family, continued the tradition of working in the store.

Young's Market, Viewed from Ardmore; Removal of Street Car Tracks and
Construction of Retaining Wall on Arlington Avenue in Foreground, 1954
Photo by Louis L. Stein

Ben Young, who died in 1994, was more than just the familiar tall, thin, apron-clad grocer, with his characteristic handle-bar mustache, seen regularly minding the store. He also served the community as a volunteer fireman and, for over 40 years, as a Director on the Kensington Fire District Board.

The butcher shop within Young's market was started by two brothers, Harold and George Napolitano. Following their retirement, Harold's son Gordy and his Uncle Ray bought the shop. The family has continued to lease the space in Young's Market for over 60 years, and their fresh meat still comes from the same

C&M Meat Company Harold and George patronized so many years ago.

In the midst of World War II, Hagstrom's Market was built at the southeast corner of Arlington and Amherst Avenues opposite the Pharmacy. Glen Crupper, the grocery manager, bought the store when Hagstrom's moved out and renamed it the Kensington Market. Around 1974 Crupper sold it to a man named Patel, but by 1978 the market had gone out of business. The property was sold to William Jageman, who remodeled it in 1979-80 to house the Ace Hardware and

Kensington Market, c. 1966
Viewed from Front of Pharmacy, Looking South
Photo by Louis L. Stein

an ice cream parlor. Later, other buildings were added south of the parking lot for a veterinary clinic and miscellaneous businesses.

The 1950s saw not only new construction but also the continual shifting of businesses to better quarters. In 1970 the Fire Department, along with the Police Department, moved to new and larger quarters farther north on Arlington Avenue, and the original quaint fire building was razed. This allowed the service station to expand to its present size. The residence to the north of the station was converted into a dental office, and in 1955 two lots north of Young's Market were used for a new medical and office building. The former real estate office in the Neighborhood Center relocated to the ground level of the new building, and the barber shop moved above Young's Market. In 1975, architect John Hattam constructed a complex of new buildings, including an unusual rooftop parking area, directly north of Young's Market, to accommodate a savings and loan (now the Mechanics Bank), a flower shop, and a delicatessen. The most recent commercial building on the Arlington is architect Bart Jones' office building, artfully constructed among the trees in the triangular lot between Arlington and Ardmore in 1982.

Arlington Ace Hardware, 1999
Same View as Kensington Market Photo above

While the Arlington shopping center was being developed in the late 1920s and early 1930s, another shopping district was coalescing around Colusa Circle, the intersection of Colusa, Oak View, and Berkeley Park Boulevard. Many of the early Mediterranean and Craftsman style homes in this neighborhood date from the 1920s. The area was accessible by public transportation one block away on Santa Fe Avenue and had, from the beginning, a closer tie to Berkeley than to upper Kensington.

By 1930 there were at least a dozen businesses operating in the vicinity of the Circle. A grocery store, gas station, and other small shops catered to nearby residents of Kensington and the adjacent areas of Berkeley, Albany, and El Cerrito. The cluster of four shops at 372-380 Colusa had already been built, and it is likely that three separate businesses occupied the turreted building at 1568 Oak View, currently a restaurant. The Thousand Oaks Creamery at 1540 Oak View in 1936 and the Mira Vista Creamery at 1550 Oak View in 1939 processed milk from local dairies, provided home deliveries, and operated an ice cream fountain.

By the 1940s Colusa Circle was a thriving business center. The number of businesses had increased to approximately 20, rivaling the number of businesses operating along the Arlington. There were at least two gas stations, two or three grocery stores (including an early Park & Shop owned by Frank Andronico), beauty parlors, a barber shop, variety store and a hardware store.

During the 1950s larger, more modern shopping areas grew up in Berkeley along Solano Avenue and in El Cerrito on San Pablo Avenue, ushering in an era of decline for smaller neighborhood shops. The commercial area at Colusa Circle fell victim to a trend of "one-stop shopping" typical of post-World War II consumption. Many of the shops closed; others opened but did not last long under competition from larger shopping developments. Three vacant shops at 1568 Oak View were combined into one space for use as a meeting place for a neighborhood church known as Berkeley Park Chapel. During the 1960s, buildings in the area had a rundown appearance, many stores had moved out, and a dilapidated gas station and garage stood on one corner.

During the 1970s the area enjoyed a gradual renewal, and shops once again began to attract larger numbers of customers. The Kensington Improvement Club (KIC) and property owners Ed Hammonds and Narsai David were the key players in the Colusa Circle resurgence. The advent in 1972 of Narsai's, a nationally acclaimed restaurant, set the tone for renewal. Ed Hammonds bought eight parcels of land around the circle, and at an open house on December 18, 1982, he revealed an ambitious four-phase $2.5 million redevelopment plan. In an effort to contribute to the enhancement of the appearance of the area, the KIC pre-vailed upon PG&E to underground the utilities around Colusa Circle. The Club also convinced the County to install a traffic island in the inter-section of the six converging streets that formed the Circle in order to increase pedestrian safety and help control traffic. Undergrounding was approved in December 1985, and work started the following year. On completion of the under-grounding, a temporary circular island was installed on a trial basis in 1986.

KIC Volunteers Install Plaque to Joseph Barnwell in Island at Colusa Circle, 1990
Photo by Natalie Salsig

Hammonds had further improved the appearance of the area by removing the dilapi-dated garage and service stations on property he had purchased; however, his redevelopment plans were not embraced by neighborhood resi-dents who considered the plans to be an overde-velopment of the property and feared the result-ing traffic congestion and parking problems would jeopardize their residential neighbor-hoods. Legal action was brought against Ham-monds to stop the project; and although the State Court of Appeals ruled in his favor in 1986, as a result of widespread local opposition, only Phase I of the plan was completed in 1987.

Removal of the utility poles surrounding Colusa Circle was completed in 1988, and a per-manent oval-shaped traffic island was installed.

Plaque to Joseph Barnwell on Boulder in Colusa Circle
Photo by Paul Lettieri

Kensington landscape architect Ted Osmundson volunteered to design the island, its landscape, and its irrigation system. The Kensington Improvement Club paid for the installation of automatic sprinklers and landscaping. Volunteers from the Club did the planting under the direction of Osmundson in the spring of 1989. The island was dedicated to Joe Barnwell, a former member of the KIC, who made the first measurements for the circle.

Trompe l'Oeil by John Wehrle on Wall of Shop on Colusa Avenue. Note Circle's Cat on Window Ledge, 1999
Photo by Paul Lettieri

Today, Colusa Circle presents a beautiful entrance to Kensington and once again offers a thriving collection of restaurants, unique shops, and small businesses, including a haberdashery that claims to be the only store in America to sell nothing but men's vintage clothing; the popular Kensington Circus, an "authentic" British pub; Semifreddi's Bakery, which started in Kensington in 1984 as a small neighborhood bakery but expanded over the years to fame and other locations; Doug Green's clock shop; Catharine Hiersoux Ceramics; and last but not least, the Circle's cat, known alternately as "44" or "Ford." Although Narsai David's restaurant has closed, he still has an office above the pub.

Since the rapid development of the late 1920s to 1950s, the size of Kensington's obvious commercial community has remained relatively fixed, clustered around the upper hub at Arlington and Amherst Avenues and the lower hub at Colusa Circle. Other less apparent changes have nevertheless occurred in the business community. One of the more influential developments has been the shift to a computer-driven economy, which made it possible for many small businesses to operate entirely out of home offices. In addition to these newer technology-based businesses, Kensington has long had a complement of artists and craftspeople working in home studios.

In an effort to increase public awareness of the quantity and quality of the many businesses and professional services available in Kensington, a handful of local entrepreneurs formed the Kensington Business and Professional Association (KBPA) in 1977. As a service to the community, the KBPA published the Kensington Business and Service Directory, which identified over 120 businesses, artists, free-lancers, and professionals operating in Kensington. In 1996 the organization's mission statement referred to "the over 150 businesses and professionals who consider themselves an integral part of the community."

Many of Kensington's current businesses are home-based. While the actual number of such businesses is unknown, 28% (nearly 400) respondents to the KIC

1995 Questionnaire reported they work at home at least part-time. This figure presumably includes employees of non-resident firms who telecommute on a full or part-time basis. Whatever the true number of independent hidden entrepreneurs, for the most part it appears that these "cottage industries" are not dependent on local patronage for their success because virtually none reported a significant proportion of clients or customers among local residents. Moreover, more than half the Questionnaire respondents indicated they do less than ten percent of their daily shopping in Kensington.

* * *

The history of Kensington is one of a unique cohesive community with a rich history of independence and a remarkable involvement of its citizenry in affairs that affect their community. In contrast to surrounding areas, Kensington has managed to retain much of its village-like atmosphere and small town charm while still enjoying the cultural advantages of a surrounding metropolis. The history of Kensington has been, if anything, the story of efforts to retain that flavor.

Streetcar on Arlington Avenue, Looking North
Photo Taken from Location of Existing Bus Stop, c. 1912
Photo by Louis L. Stein

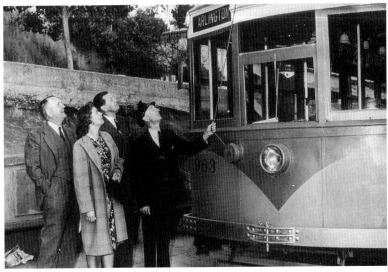

The Last #7 Streetcar, June 1948
Louis Stein at Far Left
Photo by Louis L. Stein

SOURCES

Berkeley History Center files.

"Blake Estate Oral History Project," 1986-87, Bancroft Library, UC Berkeley.

"Blake Estate, Kensington, California," Department of Landscape Architecture, UC Berkeley.

Cardwell, Kenneth H. *Bernard Maybeck: Artisan, Architect, Artist*. Salt Lake City: Peregrine Smith, 1983.

Carroll, Jonathan. *The Suburbs of San Francisco (East Bay)*. San Francisco: Chronicle Books, 1969.

Cerny, Susan S. Stern. *Northside: Historic Survey of a North Berkeley Neighborhood Before and After the 1923 Wildfire*. Berkeley Architectural Heritage Association, 1990.

Concus, Celia, Interviews with people knowledgeable about Kensington's history, including Earl Ramer, Dave Sugarbaker, Louis Stein, Janet Stein Wright, Howard and Carol Kirk, Josef Novitzky, Gladys Mea, Ben Berke, Narsai David, Paul Kieser.

Contra Costa County Assessor's Office files.

"Contra Costa County Cities and Towns," *North News*, 4/16/75.

Emanuels, George. *California's Contra Costa County, an Illustrated History*.

"Fellowship House: Fifty Years of Growth." Author and date unknown.

Gudde, Erwin G. *California Place Names*. University of California Press, 1969.

Handbook of North American Indians, Vol. VIII. Smithsonian Institution, 1978.

Kelts' Geographical Directory, March 1936.

Kensington Business and Professional Association. *Kensington Business & Service Directory*. 1992.

Kensington Improvement Club. *A Survey of Kensington*, 1978.

Kensington Improvement Club 1995 Questionnaire data.

Kensington Outlook, November 1992.

Kingsley, Madeline, Interviews with local residents and business owners, including
    Yvonne Young, Gordy Napolitano, and Steve Gaustad, 1996.

League of Women Voters (Richmond), *Know Your Town*, 1966.

Margolin, Malcolm. *The Ohlone Way; Indian Life in the San Francisco/ Monterey
    Bay Area*. Heyday Press, 1978.

Milliken, Randall. *A Time of Little Choice: The Disintegration of Tribal Culture in the San
    Francisco Bay Area, 1769-1810*. Ballena Press, 1995.

Staniford, Edward. *El Cerrito, Historical Evolution*. El Cerrito-Kensington
    Bicentennial Committee, 1976.

West County Times: 4/16/75, 2/6/88, 2/4/89, 8/1/93, 3/2/97.

Wilson, Mark A. *East Bay Heritage: A Potpourri of Living History*. San Francisco:
    California Living Books, 1979.

Woodbridge, Sally. *Maybeck: A Visionary Architect*. New York: Abbieville, 1996.

Site of Future Mechanics Bank Building
Looking South toward Young's Market
Photo by Louis L. Stein

Horse Drawn Wagon in Front of Pharmacy
Photo by Louis L. Stein

GOVERNMENT AND PUBLIC SERVICES

3

K ensington is an unincorporated area of Contra Costa County. As a consequence, governmental services are fragmented among county offices, agencies and districts, regional districts, and local independent special districts. This unique governmental structure is the result of a political decision made in 1917 by the County Board of Supervisors, when residents in the area around what is now El Cerrito and Kensington were contemplating incorporation. As a compromise between the "town" residents in the El Cerrito area and the dairy farmers in the Kensington hillside area, who strongly opposed becoming a part of a city, the Supervisors drew the boundaries of the proposed city to exclude the areas of opposition. This action left Kensington an unincorporated pocket of land under the jurisdiction of the County.

During the intervening years, Kensington residents have made four attempts to change their form of local government. In 1957 and again in 1982, efforts were made to incorporate Kensington as a city. Both times incorporation was defeated by a wide margin. Attempts to annex Kensington to El Cerrito were also defeated in 1956 and 1966. As a result of these decisions, Kensington has remained unincorporated. What Kensington gained was the freedom from city politics and bureaucracy. What it failed to gain was local control over services such as public works and planning matters, including building and second unit applications, variances, and code enforcement. While many residents feel being unincorporated has disadvantages, others feel it is a small price to pay for the independence it offers.

In order to understand Kensington's status as an unincorporated area, it is necessary to have a clear picture of the economic constraints imposed on counties by the state and federal governments which, in turn, affect the ability of the county to provide the level of service Kensington residents expect. For many years Contra Costa County has suffered from the continued erosion of state and federal aid to counties. This erosion is vividly evident in Chart 1, which shows that 61% of the County's general purpose revenue came from state and federal aid in

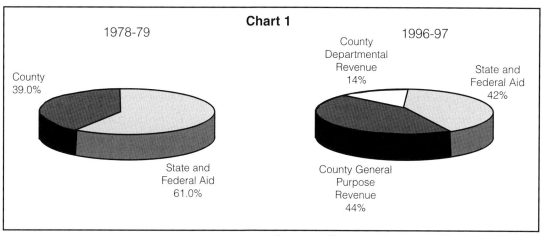

Chart 1

1978-79

County
39.0%

State and
Federal Aid
61.0%

1996-97

County
Departmental
Revenue
14%

State and
Federal Aid
42%

County General
Purpose
Revenue
44%

Erosion of State and Federal Aid in County Budget
1978-79 Compared to 1996-1997
Source: Gus Kramer County Assessor, 3/10/97

1978-79, compared to only 42% in 1996-97. This statewide decrease in funding to the County filters down to a decrease in money available to unincorporated areas within the County.

Furthermore, beginning in 1992-93, the State shifted over $3 billion in property taxes from the counties, special districts, and cities to the schools. This seizure of county property tax revenues resulted in a loss of $81.5 million to Contra Costa County in 1994-95 and dramatically reduced available funding to special districts. The result was substantial revenue constraints faced by Kensington's fire and police departments.

In addition, as a result of the restrictive provisions in Proposition 13 regarding property tax distributions, Contra Costa County faces a financial limitation not experienced by other counties. Prior to Proposition 13, the County Supervisors set the property tax rate. Proposition 13 froze these rates at

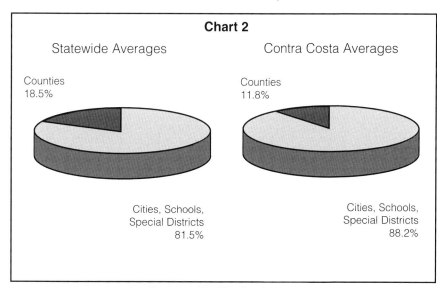

Chart 2

Statewide Averages

Counties
18.5%

Cities, Schools,
Special Districts
81.5%

Contra Costa Averages

Counties
11.8%

Cities, Schools,
Special Districts
88.2%

Property Tax Distribution, 1996-1997

their current levels in 1978. Unfortunately, because the rates in effect in Contra Costa County at that time were lower than average, the County suffered a severe financial disadvantage over the ensuing years. Whereas in the fiscal 1996-97 year, the average county received 18.5% of the property tax distribution, Contra Costa County received only 11.8% (see Chart 2). This lower property tax share cost the county $43.8 million in 1996-97. Moreover, these losses were exacerbated by a decline in the growth of assessed valuation. A 1992 attempt by the Supervisors to raise revenues by parcel tax assessments failed to get the necessary two-thirds vote from the electorate. Property tax revenues are generally allocated as follows: County 12%, Cities 8%, Schools 51%, Independent Special Districts 12%, County Districts 8%, Redevelopment Agencies 8%, Libraries 1%.

Sales tax is a major source of revenue for the state and cities, but not for counties. The largest recipient of sales tax is the state, followed by cities, which receive large amounts due to their automotive, retail, and regional shopping bases. The irony is that although only the counties provide regional services, they do so without benefit of an equitable share of regional revenue. Chart 3, on the distribution of sales tax in 1996-97, shows Contra Costa County received only 9% of the local one-cent tax, while cities within the county received 91%.

In addition to economic constraints, the services Kensington receives from the County are adversely affected by its small size and inconvenient location with respect to its governing body. Located in the farthest corner of the County, 25 miles from the County seat in Martinez, Kensington is easy for county agencies to ignore, and the community's voice often goes unheard.

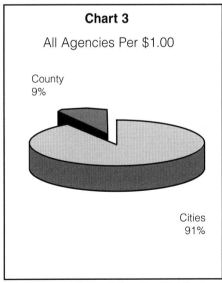

Chart 3

All Agencies Per $1.00

County
9%

Cities
91%

Contra Costa Sales Tax Distribution,
1996-1997

STRUCTURE OF KENSINGTON'S GOVERNMENT

Contra Costa County's five-person Board of Supervisors is the governing body for Kensington. In addition, some of Kensington's services are controlled by regional districts and some by local independent special districts. The County is divided into five supervisorial districts, each supervised by one member of the Board. Kensington is part of District I, along with El Cerrito, Richmond, San Pablo, North Richmond, and parts of El Sobrante and Pinole.

I. SERVICES PROVIDED BY THE COUNTY

(Only divisions of Contra Costa County government pertaining to Kensington are listed.)

A. Administration
1. Contra Costa County Board of Supervisors
2. County Administrator
3. Assessor
4. Auditor-Controller
5. Treasurer-Tax Collector
6. Clerk-Recorder

B. Public Protection
1. Courts (Superior Court, Municipal Courts)
2. District Attorney-Public Administrator
3. Sheriff-Coroner
4. Public Defender
5. County Probation Officer
6. Grand Jury

C. Public Services
1. Social Services Department
2. Health Services Department
3. Veterans' Service Officer
4. Animal Control (including the Animal Service Center in Pinole)
5. Agricultural Law Enforcement
6. Division of Weights and Measures

D. Community Development Department
   (Planning and land development)

E. Building Inspection Department

F. Public Works Department

G. Education
   1. County Superintendent of Schools
   2. County Board of Education

H. Library Services
   1. Kensington Branch Library
   2. Contra Costa Central Library Reference Service

I. Service Area L-100 Lighting District
   (Street lighting is maintained by a county contract with PG&E)

J. LL2 Landscape District Z-21

II. REGIONAL DISTRICTS PROVIDING SERVICES (partial listing)

A. The Alameda-Contra Costa Transit District

B. The Bay Area Rapid Transit District (BART)

C. The East Bay Municipal Utility District

D. The East Bay Regional Park District

E. The Bay Area Air Quality Management District

F. The Association of Bay Area Governments

III. SERVICES PROVIDED BY LOCAL INDEPENDENT SPECIAL DISTRICTS

A. Kensington Fire Protection District
1. Fire Protection Services
2. Fire Prevention Services
3. Medical Emergency Services
4. Disaster Preparedness Services
5. Public Assistance including Rescue and Extrication Services
6. Public Education and Training Classes

B. Kensington Police Protection and Community Services District
1. Police Protection Services
2. Traffic Safety
3. Parks and Recreation
4. Refuse Collection

C. Stege Sanitary District
1. Sewage Collection and Transfer System Services

Kensington is not completely without local government. Two independent special districts have been created by a vote of Kensington residents, the Kensington Fire Protection District (KFPD) and the Kensington Police Protection and Community Services District (KCSD).

What is a special district? A special district is created by a vote of the residents who live within the boundaries of the proposed district and is sanctioned by an act of the State Legislature under specific government codes. There are two kinds of special districts, dependent and independent. A dependent district is governed by the County Board of Supervisors, while an independent district is a self-governed agency administered by a locally approved board of directors. Services provided by a special district are as diverse as services provided by any other public agency. Because the districts operate locally, they can respond quickly to the needs of local residents through direct accessibility.

Both the KFPD and the KCSD are independent districts, formed in 1937 and 1953 respectively by Kensington voters to provide local services. Each is an independent self-governed agency responsible directly to its constituents, and each is administered by a local board of five directors elected by Kensington voters. Services provided by the KFPD and the KCSD are primarily funded by property taxes allocated by the County and supplemented by a special tax approved by voters.

The Stege Sanitary District is also a special district; however, its services cover more than just the Kensington area. In addition to these special districts, the Kensington Municipal Advisory Council (KMAC) provides input to the County Community Development Department on variances and land use applications.

Residents who responded to the KIC 1995 Questionnaire appear to favor the current taxation arrangement. Of the 1,409 respondents, 56% expressed satisfaction or strong satisfaction with the system, while 17% were dissatisfied or strongly dissatisfied. Twenty-six percent were either neutral or declined to answer the question. It is interesting to note, however, that even though 17% of the respondents appear to object to the current system of raising funds for special districts, it is clear that respondents are not dissatisfied in general with the services provided by the districts to which these funds are directed.

THE KENSINGTON FIRE PROTECTION DISTRICT

The Kensington Fire Protection District is one of three Independent Fire Districts in the County. The District is governed by a five-person Board of Directors elected by Kensington voters for a term of four years. Board meetings are held monthly, and directors are not compensated. The District provides a full range of fire protection and medical and emergency services (including fire suppression, rescue, extrication, and public assistance) as well as disaster preparedness services. The District serves the community through an engine company stationed at the Kensington fire house on Arlington Avenue, which operates under a contract for fire service with the City of El Cerrito.

The engine company is staffed by a crew of three firefighters 24 hours a day. Dispatching services are provided by the City of Richmond. The majority of calls for service in Kensington are for medical emergencies and other types of emergency public assistance. The department prides itself on an emergency response time of six minutes or less for 95% of emergency calls.

Kensington Fire House, 1975
Photo by Louis L. Stein

Funding for the District is derived from county-allocated property taxes supplemented by a special tax in an amount voted by residents, currently $83 annually per residential parcel. The operating budget for 1999-2000 is approximately $1.3 million. The District owns the public safety building at 217 Arlington Avenue, which also houses the Kensington Police Department. Rolling stock consists of an International Pumper engine and a 1998 Type Four Patrol fire engine.

The Kensington and El Cerrito fire departments have had a shared arrangement for directing fire fighting and life saving operations since the 1970s. The Kensington Fire Protection District also participates with other West County fire agencies in automatic response agreements that use the combined resources of all agencies to serve the area irrespective of jurisdictional lines. Reciprocity of services is ensured by meeting common staffing, training, and equipment standards. The District also has a Mutual Response Area (MRA) agreement with the cities of Berkeley, El Cerrito, Richmond, the East Bay Regional Park District, and the Contra Costa County Fire Protection District to provide enhanced fire protection on critical fire hazard days along the ridge line from the Alameda County line north to McBryde Avenue in Richmond. The MRA is initiated on "Red Flag Warning" days when fire danger is extreme. Any report of fire occurring within the boundary of the MRA will generate the enhanced response.

In 1996, the Fire Department initiated a fire hazard abatement program to eliminate fire hazards in the community by removing refuse and vegetation that is dry, dead, easily ignited, and capable of spreading fire rapidly, thereby causing damage to structures and endangering lives. Each spring the Department draws up a list of properties that constitute the greatest fire hazards. The owner is notified that unless the hazardous conditions are corrected, the Fire Department will abate the public nuisance, and the cost of abatement will be assessed against the property as a special assessment. A hearing is held at which the property owner may object to the fire hazard designation and order to abate. Voluntary compliance by residents has been outstanding.

A fire prevention program is also in force, with particular emphasis on aggressive fuel management to prevent a wildland/urban interface conflagration. Classes in fire safety and prevention, first aid, and various phases of emergency preparedness are held at the Kensington Community Center or in El Cerrito. In addition, home safety inspection services are available through the Fire Department.

The Kensington Fire Department was established on May 5, 1928, by the County Board of Supervisors under Health and Safety Code 13-801. Three Fire Commissioners, Donald H. Parce, John L. Mason, and W. G. Foster, were appointed to administer the new District. The original station was located in the former Neighborhood Center, in a small, quaint, French country-style building designed by local architect W. R. Yelland, on property now occupied by the Chevron service station. In 1934 Fred Wallis, the owner of the small gas station adjacent to the station, was hired as the first Fire Chief. Albert Stein, father of Louis Stein, then owner of the Arlington Pharmacy, was the night man.

In 1937, by an act of the State Legislature, the Fire Department was made an Independent Special District. Until 1952, the Department was staffed by volunteers (sometimes as many as 25), most of whom rushed to the station from their jobs in Kensington to man the truck when the alarm sounded. They were assisted by "student sleepers" who lived at the firehouse while attending classes at UC. The Volunteer Firefighter Association continued to supplement the Department until 1987, by which time the staff of paid personnel had grown to 14.

By the late 1960s the department had outgrown its small building, and the hillside foundation of the building was showing signs of erosion. In 1969 bonds were passed to fund a new building to be constructed on two lots purchased by the District in 1947 at 217 Arlington Avenue. The new building was occupied in 1970.

By the 1980s fire suppression services were becoming more complex and rigorous while revenue allocations from the state and county were becoming more uncertain. It was also increasingly apparent that more interaction and mutual aid were necessary to ensure safety for all communities. The Kensington Fire Department developed reciprocal agreements with neighboring jurisdictions as well as an operational agreement with El Cerrito that permitted both departments to operate as one for training purposes and fire response. The name of the District was changed to the Kensington Fire Protection District to comply with the Bergeson Fire Protection law of 1987 (Health and Safety Code 13800).

Several events occurred in the 1990s that would produce major changes in the way the Fire Department operated. Mounting public dissatisfaction with high budget requirements and management problems within the District prompted an audit of the Department in 1993 by the Kensington Property Owners Association. The report was critical of management and of the expenditure of funds. In addition, state legislation had resulted in a loss to special districts of post-Proposition 13 bail-out funds, and the amount of funding from property tax revenues was in jeopardy. Moreover, there was mounting pressure from the county for "functional integration" or consolidation of fire departments throughout the county. The survival of a small independent district like Kensington looked bleak.

Three choices were available to the Board of Directors to address the issue: (1) continue operations by reducing staff and eliminating the position of Fire Chief; (2) consolidate operations with the County and thereby lose local control of the District; or (3) contract for services with another agency but retain local control of the District's administration.

In 1993 the Fire Board Directors solicited proposals from Berkeley, El Cerrito, and the County to determine the feasibility of contracting. At the same time, the Kensington Fire Chief, Sam Treese, retired on disability. Vic Porter, a retired Berkeley Fire Chief, was hired as a consultant to help evaluate contracting proposals and to work with Battalion Chief Jim Gozzano to keep the Fire Department operating.

In 1994 the Board of Directors was increased from three to five members, and in 1995 a contract for operational services was signed with the City of El Cerrito. The contract allowed the Kensington Fire District to reduce its budget by some $400,000, to preserve its independent Special District status, and to continue administering the District through its local Board of Directors.

The 1995 Kensington Improvement Club Questionnaire asked residents how they felt about the Kensington Fire District. Of the 1,409 responses, 1,138 (81%) were either very satisfied or satisfied, 125 (9%) were neutral, and only 120 (9%) expressed dissatisfaction.

KENSINGTON POLICE PROTECTION AND COMMUNITY SERVICES DISTRICT

The Kensington Community Services District (KCSD) was formed as an Independent Special District in 1953 under State Government Code 60,100-61,749 to exercise police powers in Kensington. In 1993 the name of the District was changed to the Kensington Police Protection and Community Services District to assure qualification for special state funding to police districts; however, the district is still referred to locally as KCSD. The District employs a Police Chief who also serves as District General Manager, a force of nine officers, a part-time secretary, a custodian, and gardening help.

The KCSD is administered by a five-person unpaid Board of Directors elected for staggered four-year terms. Board meetings are held monthly. The District owns the Community Center building and grounds, the Annex, Kensington Park, Building E, and one-half of the parking lot located north of the library. It also owns the triangular lot between Arlington Avenue and Coventry Road.

The KCSD operating budget for 1999-2000 is approximately $1.18 million. The budget is primarily funded by property tax revenues and a voter-approved annual $300 special residential parcel tax. Dispatching services for the police, originally provided by El Cerrito and later by Albany, were transferred to

Richmond in 1993 as part of a West Contra Costa County plan to consolidate all dispatching services. The Police Department has mutual aid agreements with cities in Alameda and Contra Costa Counties, the East Bay Regional Park District, and the State of California. The police caseload each year includes approximately 2,000 "numbered cases" (crimes) and more than 2,000 miscellaneous public service cases. The District owns five police cars, and streets are patrolled around the clock.

Before 1946 Kensington had no police department. The Berkeley Police patrolled up to the county line, but no farther. Contra Costa County would respond in due time from Martinez, but not soon enough to protect Kensington in an emergency. The Machell Police Patrol provided some services to the Kensington area in the early 1930s, but little is known about it. The first paid policeman was hired in 1935 when a Mr. Fred Norton agreed to patrol the area. He furnished his own automobile, a Model T Ford, and each household contributed $1.00-$1.50 per month to pay his salary.

In 1946, at the end of World War II, the community voted to form a Police Protection Unit and hired patrolmen who cruised in their own cars. At first it was only a two-man force consisting of Chief Alton Bowley and officer Rolf Hagen, supplemented by volunteers. The first official traffic citation was issued on May 1, 1947. In 1949 the Unit bought its own police cars, and in 1950 Chief Bowley was succeeded by Chief James Kendrick.

In 1953 the Police Protection Unit was replaced by the Kensington Community Services District. A three-person Board of Directors was elected to govern the District, and George Yool became Police Chief, a position he held for nearly twenty years. By 1957 the number of patrolmen had been increased to five, and Louise Farley was hired as secretary. In 1995 the Board was expanded from three to five members.

Beginning in the mid-forties, the Police Department was located in the building at 264 Arlington Avenue owned by realtor Stan Roth. In 1970, when the Kensington Fire Department constructed a new public safety building, space on the second floor was leased to the Police Department.

Louis Stein Receives the First Traffic Citation Issued by Chief A. F. Bowley of the Kensington Police, May 1, 1947

In 1999, the building was remodeled to allow space on the ground floor for the Department.

In 1955 residents voted to add park and recreation responsibilities to the KCSD. The District contracts with the Kensington Community Council (KCC), a non-profit volunteer corporation, to administer the recreation program. The Council also contributes some funds for construction and maintenance of facilities and provides citizen input on recreational needs. The KCC has no governmental powers and receives no tax support.

In 1979, by public vote, the authority to administer the franchise for refuse collection in Kensington was vested in the KCSD. This continued until 1996 when the refuse company with whom the District had contracted for service requested the County Board of Supervisors take over the unexpired contract following a dispute with the District over a proposed 11% rate increase. This action resulted in a lawsuit filed by the District against the Board of Supervisors challenging its right to take over Kensington's exercise of statutory authority for solid waste matters, as well as its right to nullify Kensington's existing franchise agreement with the refuse company. The suit was dropped in 1997 when the County agreed to return the administration of the franchise to the KCSD.

In 1995 the KCSD issued bonds to purchase the last eight acres of land that it did not already own in the Kensington Park area from the West Contra Costa Unified School District. A Kensington Park Advisory Committee was appointed to draw up a comprehensive plan for the future development of the park land. The plan was adopted by the KCSD Board of Directors in November 1997.

The KCSD has always had a close working relationship with, and received strong support from, the community. The high visibility of patrol cars day and night has been a strong deterrent to crime. Effective October 1, 1997, a community policing program was put into effect for the purpose of creating a positive interaction and ongoing relationship between residents and officers, assisting residents in crime prevention, and determining the causes of and solutions to perceived local problems. Three community policing teams were appointed, consisting of one sergeant and two police officers per team. Each team is responsible for a particular neighborhood assignment, including going door-to-door to meet residents of the neighborhood. In 1999 a Reserve Police Officer Program was initiated to supplement and assist the paid force.

A question in the 1995 Kensington Questionnaire regarding satisfaction with services provided by Kensington's local districts indicated that 84% of the 1,409 respondents were very satisfied or satisfied with the KCSD. Only 3% expressed dissatisfaction. The following statement made by one respondent was echoed in many of the comments included with the Questionnaire: "The services we get are well worth the cost."

KENSINGTON EMERGENCY PREPAREDNESS COUNCIL

Kensington: "a peaceful hideaway in the midst of urban madness," "the almost perfect place to live," "a small safe community of educated and concerned citizens," ". . . safe, peaceful, serene." These were some of the descriptions of Kensington in answer to the request in the 1995 KIC Questionnaire to provide an image of Kensington in a short phrase.

A different image given was, "a relatively safe community poised on the Hayward Fault, which makes us nervous." That same nervousness was reflected by 94% of the 1,409 Kensington residents who responded to the Questionnaire. Seven hundred fifty-three respondents stated they were "very concerned" over potential earthquake damage, and 572 said they were "somewhat concerned." Only 37 of those responding expressed no concern.

The same degree of concern, coupled with memories of the destruction caused by the 1989 Loma Prieta earthquake, provided the incentive for the KIC to initiate a study of the status of community emergency preparedness and to ask, "just how prepared is Kensington for a natural disaster which could strike at any time?"

The KIC study began in late 1989 with a review of the County "Multi-Hazard Functional Plan," which revealed the County had given little or no attention to emergency planning in Kensington. In 1990, the KIC requested that the County Board of Supervisors revise the plan to include provisions for the community. A new section entitled "The Kensington Community Insert" was completed in September 1990. The result, however, contained inaccurate information and was too broad in scope to be of any practical use.

It was obvious that, like so many other issues the community has faced, emergency preparedness, if addressed at all, was destined to become a do-it-yourself project.

In 1991 the KIC compiled and distributed a booklet titled "There's An Earthquake In Your Future - Are You Ready For It?" The booklet was partially financed by a $5,000 grant from Shearson Lehman obtained through the efforts of former County Supervisor Tom Powers. In addition, the KIC initiated a

Neighborhood Emergency Preparedness Program in which blocks of homes were organized into self-help teams and instructed in first aid and other survival skills. The program met with limited success. The 1995 Questionnaire asked the question, "Have you made any preparations for earthquake survival?" Of the 1,409 responses, 1,071 (76%) answered yes, and 278 (20%) said no.

However real the prospects of a devastating earthquake in the near future appear, many residents consider vulnerability to wildfire an even greater threat to their "small safe community." Of the 1,409 responses to the KIC Questionnaire, almost half (692) were "very concerned," and 624 (40%) were "somewhat concerned." Only 59 were "not at all concerned." The 1991 Oakland firestorm was a wake-up call to the dangers inherent in a community such as Kensington, with its wildland interface, narrow winding streets, unmanaged vegetation, and love of shake roofs. Fire could come from the wildland interface to the east, along the ridge lines north and south of the community, or from the "urban forest" within Kensington. The sobering fact is that this community is every bit as vulnerable to a wildfire as the Oakland hill area.

In 1992 the Kensington Improvement Club addressed the issue of fire safety in a document submitted to the Fire and Police Departments titled "Making Kensington More Firesafe." The document urged the departments to work with community groups to identify an appropriate fire protection strategy for Kensington. It suggested specific elements to be included in the strategy and recommendations for mitigating the hazards involved. Although some of the recommendations were implemented, the response was minimal.

In 1995, after the Kensington Fire District signed a contract for fire service with the City of El Cerrito, a joint Emergency Preparedness Council (EPC) was formed with the KCSD. The Council membership includes two members from each of the KFPD and KCSD Boards. The Fire and Police Chiefs provide staff assistance. Kensington now has, for the first time, an official body to address emergency preparedness in a comprehensive manner.

The mission of the EPC is to develop a plan to enhance the community's ability to respond to and recover from a disaster in an organized manner; to mobilize resources consistent with the State of California Standardized Emergency Management System (SEMS); and to explore and employ effective mitigation strategies such as communication and warning systems, plans for care and shelter, plans for evacuation and emergency access, and fuel management.

SEMS establishes the chain of communication from Kensington, via the El Cerrito Communication Center, to the County and State Offices of Emergency Services. To facilitate this communication, the EPC has established sites for five emergency communication centers in Kensington. These centers are supplied with amateur radio equipment and, during an emergency, will be staffed by licensed operators from the Kensington Amateur Radio Operators organization (KARO). KARO is a recently organized group of amateur radio operators who live in Kensington and volunteer their services to provide an emergency communication line for Kensington during a disaster when other lines might not be operable. The group meets monthly for training and drills, and is an integral part of the Neighborhood Emergency Assistance Team (NEAT) program.

It is important to recognize that although Kensington has mutual aid agreements with surrounding communities, the Kensington Police and Fire Departments are charged with initial response during an emergency. In the event of a widespread disaster, outside assistance could take up to 72 hours to arrive.

To meet the need for individual and neighborhood self-sufficiency during this 72-hour period, the EPC replaced the existing Neighborhood Block program with El Cerrito's NEAT program, which became available to Kensington under the provisions of the contract for service with El Cerrito. The NEAT program provides an increased level of community and neighborhood self-sufficiency by developing independent multi-functional neighborhood teams and training them in skills such as basic fire and hazard control, first aid, damage assessment, search and rescue, communications, sheltering, and special needs. These courses are designed to assist individuals to help themselves and their neighbors survive and recover from a major disaster. In the fall of 1997, the NEAT training classes were redesigned into a modular program. The new program teaches essential preparedness skills in a four-week comprehensive course including a final "hands on" skill session. Participants are required to take the entire series of classes.

The NEAT program is planned to complement professional emergency services. Each participating neighborhood is under the leadership of a block captain and one or more assistants. Homes are provided with an inventory of neighborhood skills and equipment available in an emergency, the location of the gas and electric shutoffs for each house, and contact numbers for all neighbors. Every neighborhood organized under the NEAT program will have the organizational and functional capability to survive the initial 72-hour period following a disaster and to begin recovery in the post-disaster environment. The NEAT program provides information and organizational skills that can also be useful in smaller scale emergencies such as long power outages and flooding.

When asked in the 1995 Questionnaire, "Have you joined any neighborhood groups concerned with disaster preparedness?" (Question 23), the majority (68%) had not. Of the 1,409 respondents, only 28% had joined a group. However, Question 24, which asks, "Would you be interested in joining such a neighborhood group?" reveals that 40% of those who had not joined a group would like to join. Only 30% indicated no interest in joining. These statistics show the need for expansion of the NEAT program into more neighborhoods. More volunteer effort is needed, more block captains must be recruited, and the education program must be expanded before we can rest assured that Kensington residents have the skills to survive the first 72 hours following a disaster.

Major concerns under study or still to be addressed include:
- Installing an emergency warning system
- Planning for evacuation and emergency access
- Facilitating emergency vehicle response in a disaster by reducing parking on narrow streets
- Planning for care and shelter
- Undergrounding utilities to reduce fire and safety hazards

In the responses to questions regarding undergrounding utilities in the 1995 Questionnaire, 594 (42%) indicated that the community should place a great deal of emphasis on developing plans to underground, 434 (30%) felt that some effort should be made, and 123 (9%) little effort. A willingness to pay between $1,000 and $5,000 for undergrounding utilities was indicated by 629 (55%) respondents; 524 (45%) would not pay anything, and 113 stated that their utilities were already underground.

Regarding planning for evacuation and emergency vehicle access, 702 (42%) respondents felt the community should place a "great deal" of emphasis on an evacuation plan, 509 (36%) said "some" emphasis, and 33 (less than 7%) said none.

In January 1995 Kensington was designated a Very High Fire Hazard Severity Zone (VHFHSZ) by the California Department of Forestry. Under State Law

AB337 (the Bates Bill) property owners within this zone must take special precautions, including vegetation management, to reduce the risk of fire. To comply with the law, the KFPD established fire hazard reduction vegetation management standards for private property. The goals of these standards are to keep all fires small, to limit the speed with which a fire will grow, and to make it more difficult for fires to ignite and spread. Enforcement of the following standards and abatement proceedings began in May 1996:

- A defensible 30-foot "fire break" must be created and maintained in all areas within 30 feet of any occupied dwelling. Ornamental landscaping consisting of fire resistive plants is permitted and encouraged in this area if it is well irrigated, pruned, and maintained free of dead material.
- A "fuel break" must be created and maintained in areas extending from 30 to 100 feet surrounding any structure. These are meant to deny any fire approaching the area sufficient fuel to sustain fire intensity and speed before it enters the fire break. In this area dry grass and weeds are to be maintained at a height not to exceed six inches.
- Spark arrestors must be installed on every chimney.
- A Class B or better fire resistive roof must be used on all new construction or roof replacement of over 50%.
- Property owners must maintain their property free from all nuisances including garbage, debris, rubbish and trash, hazardous materials, junk, and noxious growth.

The spirit of neighbor-helping-neighbor fostered by widespread citizen involvement, compliance, and cooperation with these fire and earthquake preparedness programs can save lives. Kensington's tradition of volunteerism and fierce independence, the qualities that make it hard for us to fit easily into a governmental niche, can help us to survive a natural disaster in our community — a wildfire, or "the big one."

KENSINGTON MUNICIPAL ADVISORY COUNCIL

The Kensington Municipal Advisory Council (KMAC) was established in 1989 by the County Board of Supervisors. The Council consists of five members and one alternate who have resided in Kensington for at least five years prior to assuming office. Council members are appointed by the County Board of Supervisors upon recommendation of the Kensington Improvement Club, the Kensington Property Owners Association, and the Kensington Municipal Advisory Council. They serve staggered four-year terms, serve without compensation, and receive no staff support from the County.

Most of the Council's activities concern land-use planning and applications for variance and conditional use permits. When applications submitted to the County Community Development Department are forwarded to the KMAC, the Council holds an informal hearing in Kensington. The recommendation of the Council, which is advisory only, is sent to the Community Development Department. It is then up to that Department to decide whether the application is to be handled administratively or forwarded to the Zoning Administrator or the Planning Commission for a hearing. After the KMAC has made its recommendation, any citizen may request a hearing before the Zoning Administrator. Decisions of the Zoning Administrator may be appealed to the Planning Commission, and any decision of the latter may be appealed to the Board of Supervisors.

Any person may appeal if the person's property rights or property value are adversely affected and the decision does not comply with the General Plan, or if the findings of the hearing body are not supported by evidence. If pertinent information was not brought to the attention of the hearing body, a motion for reconsideration may be filed. The appeal period is ten calendar days from the date of the hearing.

The Council also advises the Board of Supervisors on land use planning matters affecting Kensington, such as land use designations, master plan amendments, environmental impact reports, and negative declarations. The Council represents the community before the Zoning Administrator, the County Planning Commission, and the County Board of Supervisors on land use, planning, and zoning matters. The Board of Supervisors is the final decision-making authority with respect to Kensington.

Responses in the KIC 1995 Questionnaire regarding satisfaction with the KMAC were less positive than those for the two local Districts. Only 30% of the 1,409 respondents expressed satisfaction with the Council. Thirty-eight percent of the respondents were neutral, but only 5% were dissatisfied. Twenty-six percent gave responses classified as "other." The number of neutral or "other" responses to the questionnaire might indicate that knowledge of the activities of the KMAC is not widespread.

THE STEGE SANITARY DISTRICT

The Stege Sanitary District, the oldest political entity in Kensington, was formed in 1913 as an independent sanitary district under the State Health and Safety Code, Section 6400. The District was named after Richard Stege, a German-born Forty-Niner who settled in El Cerrito in 1870 and became prominent in the development of the area.

The function of the District is to operate and maintain a safe, efficient, and economical sewage collection and transfer system for Kensington, El Cerrito, and Richmond Annex south of Potrero Avenue. (Maintenance of storm drains is the responsibility of the County Public Works Department.) The District has a board of five directors who are compensated and elected for staggered four-year terms. The Board meets in the Stege Sanitary District Building at 7500 Schmidt Lane in El Cerrito. The small District maintains more than 155 miles of sewer lines and serves approximately 40,000 people through 13,600 residential and commercial connections. District operating expenses are funded with the revenue sources of the District, a principal source of which is the annual sewer user charge. At present, the District maintains the lowest sewer user charge rate in the East Bay.

Since 1982, daily operations have been carried out by the West Contra Costa Sanitary District under a contract with Stege. Stege now sends its sewage to the East Bay Municipal Utility District (EBMUD) treatment plant (located at the southeastern end of the Bay Bridge in Oakland) to be treated and discharged into the Bay. Before 1972, sewage was sent to a primary treatment plant at Point Isabel. When Congress passed the Clean Water Act requiring secondary treatment of all sewage, the Point Isabel plant was phased out of daily operation, and a pumping station was built at the Point to pump Stege's sewage to a shoreline pipeline called the interceptor. The interceptor carries sewage by gravity from Stege and other Bay cities to the EBMUD treatment plant, where it receives secondary chemical treatment. The Point Isabel treatment plant is now used only during periods of wet weather when the EBMUD plant cannot handle all of the water that flows into the system. During these periods, sewage receives primary treatment only and is then discharged.

The tiny Stege District has become the first sewage district in the country to use a revolutionary new process called "pipe-bursting" to remove leaking joints. The work is needed to keep old pipes from leaking and allowing rainwater to enter during the winter. Excess water causes pipes to overflow, allowing pollution to enter the Bay. The innovative technique uses polyethylene liner pipe to completely reline old sewer pipes without digging up and replacing the existing pipe. It has the advantages of being less expensive and causing less distress to private property than conventional methods. The procedure, used in parts of El Cerrito and along Anson Way and Eureka Avenue in Kensington, is the first step in a $20 million renovation of the District's sewers set to take place over the next 20 years.

In 1979 an effort was made to reorganize Stege as a subsidiary district of El Cerrito with the City Council acting as the Board of Directors. Kensington residents were strongly opposed to the effort on the grounds they would be disenfranchised since they could not vote for El Cerrito City Council members. The measure was defeated when Kensington voters turned out en masse, while voters in El Cerrito expressed indifference to the issue even though registered voters in El Cerrito outnumbered those in Kensington five to one. Richard Spellman, mayor of El Cerrito at the time, wrote in a letter to the *Outlook*, "Some residents of Kensington are disturbed at being out in the cold politically since they cannot vote for El Cerrito City Council members. I can't really believe, however, that sewers will be that hot an issue. . . ." Stege has retained its status as an Independent Special District ever since, and a lesson to be learned was: never under estimate Kensington residents when they feel strongly about an issue!

* * *

Although Berkeley borders Kensington and many residents are connected with the University of California, much of the community seems to feel little formal association with its neighboring city. On the other hand, Kensington seems only vaguely related to Contra Costa County, even though a legal

Louis Stein's PG&E Protest Banner on Arlington Pharmacy
Photo by Louis L. Stein

bond exists. In the end, Kensington's only allegiance is to itself and its desire to control its own destiny.

Residents seem to have known from the earliest days the kind of government they wanted — or didn't want — for their community. Determined to remain unincorporated, they have invented their own unique governance, tailored to their own needs and restricted to services required — no frills, no bureaucracy, no mayor, no city council — just a strong sense of community and a determination to address its needs and concerns in-house through resourcefulness and self-reliance. A strong spirit of volunteerism is the glue that holds the system together and makes it work. Kensington community leaders tackle basic issues, and community meetings provide a forum for neighborhood problem-solving and debates over local concerns. It would appear to be democracy at its best — an example of what Edmund Burke was referring to in his quotation noted on the dedication page of this book: ". . . To be attached to the subdivision, to love the little platoon we belong to in society is the first principle . . . of public affections . . . the first link in the series by which we proceed toward a love of our country and of mankind. . . ."

Kensington Fire Protection District Board Meeting, 1999
Photo by Natalie Salsig

KENSINGTON FIRE PROTECTION DISTRICT

FIRE CHIEFS

Fred Wallis	1934-1946
Gerald Lillefjeld	1946-1965
Don Markert	1965-1988
Sam Treese	1988-1993
Jim Gozzano (Interim Administrator)	1993-1995
Stephen L. Cutright	1995-1999
Mark Scott	1999-present

BOARD OF DIRECTORS

Donald H. Parce	1928-?
W.G. Foster	1928-?
John L. Mason	1928-?
Carl Day	1959-1968
Myron Bird	1959-1989
Ben Young	1965-1994
Richard Lee	1968-1980
Stuart Fletcher	1980-1983
Maurice Campbell	1983-1988
Paul Wilson	1984-1993
Martin Knight	1991-1994
Ron Egherman	1993-1996
Jim Walker	1994-1996
Chuck Grant	1994-1996
Janice Kosel	1994-present
Natalie Salsig	1994-present
Gloria Morrison	1996-present
Gilbert Bendix	1996-present
Don Dommer	1996-present

KENSINGTON POLICE PROTECTION AND COMMUNITY SERVICES DISTRICT

POLICE CHIEFS

A. F. Bowley	1947-1950
James K. Kendrick	1950-1953
George A. Yool	1953-1972
Walter E. Gist	1972-1977
Jack I. Christian	1977-1985
James M. Bray	1985-1998
Barry D. Garfield	1998-present

Kensington Police Protection and Community Services District Board Meeting, 1999

BOARD OF DIRECTORS

George F. Cake	1947-1948
James F. Wellington	1947-1953
Paul Thomas	1947-1951
Robert Claxton	1948-1953
Philip Phillips	1951-1952
Mervyn E. Abbott	1952-1953
James F. Wellington	1953-1975
Robert Claxton	1953-1957
Mervyn E. Abbott	1953-1956
Harold B. Ingold	1956-1960
Stanley Roth	1957-1966
George L. Weamer	1960-1964
Bernard E. Etcheverry	1964-1971
J. W. Otvos	1966-1972
Edward M. Hirata	1971-1985
Hugo H. Sephton	1972-1973
James W. Ogilvie	1973-1977
Dorothy J. Collins	1975-1977
Robert F. Birtcil	1977-1977
Lester K. Ellis	1977-1980
Peter D. Nussbaum	1977-1981
Lawrence S. Thal	1980-1994
Sheila P. Brody	1981-1994
John A. Pierce	1985-1996
David Anton	1995-1996
David Fike	1994-1998
Lynn Wolter	1994-1998
John Ream	1995-1998
Gail Feldman	1997-1998
Joan Gallegos	1996-present
Paul Haxo	1998-present
Patricia McLaughlin	1998-present
Bruce Morrow	1998-present
Ciara Wood	1998-present

KENSINGTON MUNICIPAL ADVISORY COUNCIL

BOARD MEMBERS

Ovid Rose	1989-1993	Marianne Loring	1992-present
Bob Hansen	1989-1990	Jim Naftzger	1994-1996
Larry Wood	1989-1993	Stephen Farneth	1996-present
Edythe Campbell	1989-1995	James Carman	1997-present
Richard Muller	1989-1997	Michael Abraham	1997-present
Barbara Miller	1990-1991	Ed Detmer	2000-present
John Grosvenor	1992-2000	Joel Turtle	2000-present

SOURCES

California Special District Report: "History of the Property Tax Shift," February 1997.

Contra Costa County Auditor Controller Report, 1990.

Emanuels, George. *California Contra Costa County: An Illustrated History*. Panorama West Books, 1986.

Kensington Community Services District News Release, 10/16/96.

Kensington Fire Department, "Fire Hazard Reduction Program," 1995.

Kensington Fire District Handbook.

Kensington Outlook: June 1993, July/August 1993; September 1993.

Kramer, Gus, County Assessor, "Assessment Information for the Contra Costa County Property Owner," 3/10/97.

Office of the County Administrator, "Efficiency and Economy in Contra Costa County Government," no date.

Richmond Independent, 5/2/57.

Salsig, Natalie, Interview with Police Chief Jim Bray, 1996.

San Francisco Chronicle, 6/97.

Stege Sanitary District, "The Endeavor," Volume VIII, #1, 1997.

COMMUNITY LIFE

4

KENSINGTON BOARDS AND ORGANIZATIONS

ELECTED OR APPOINTED (SEE "GOVERNMENT AND PUBLIC SERVICES" CHAPTER)

Kensington Fire Protection District Board of Directors

Kensington Police Protection and Community Services District
Board of Directors

Kensington Municipal Advisory Council

VOLUNTEER CIVIC ORGANIZATIONS

Kensington Improvement Club

Kensington Property Owners Association

Kensington Community Council

Friends of the Kensington Library

Kensington Business and Professional Association

Kensington Lions Club

Blakemont Property Owners Association

Kensington Amateur Radio Operators

POLITICAL ORGANIZATIONS

Kensington Area Republican Women's Club

El Cerrito Democratic Club

League of Women Voters (Kensington Unit)

SOCIAL AND CULTURAL ORGANIZATIONS

Arlington Women's Club

Kensington Seniors

Kensington Symphony Orchestra

YOUTH GROUPS

Cub Scouts

Boy Scouts of America

Brownies

Girl Scouts U.S.A.

CHURCHES

Arlington Community Church
Unitarian Universalist Church of Berkeley

SCHOOLS AND EDUCATIONAL ORGANIZATIONS
(SEE "SCHOOLS" CHAPTER)

PUBLIC

Kensington Elementary School
Kensington School PTA
Kensington Dads' Club
Kensington Education Foundation
Kensington Site Council

PRIVATE

Arlington Preschool
Claremont Day Nurseries
Golden Gate Apple School
Kensington Nursery School
Montessori Family School
Montessori School of Kensington
Neighborhood School
Skytown Parent Cooperative Preschool

Arlington Community Church and Kensington Nursery School on Arlington Avenue
Photo by Theodore Osmundson

VOLUNTEER CIVIC ORGANIZATIONS: THE "K'S" OF KENSINGTON

The introductory outline on the two preceding pages lists the many boards and organizations that contribute to community life in Kensington. The civic organizations with elected or appointed boards of directors have been discussed in previous chapters. The schools and related organizations have a chapter of their own. This chapter describes the remaining groups, the activities of which, each in their own way, enrich the community.

Earlier chapters of this book have revealed a common thread running throughout the story of Kensington's development — a strong desire by its citizens for local control over their unincorporated community and a willingness to volunteer their services to provide that control and compensate for services the town does not receive from the County. This basic "do-it-yourself" attitude accounts for the remarkable involvement and personal interest of Kensington citizens in the affairs of their community and the spirit of volunteerism that permeates every facet of community life today.

Local police and fire protection services, playgrounds, a recreation program, a park, after-school programs, town hall meetings, a community newspaper, a library, parades, a second unit ordinance, civic improvement activities, a symphony, and emergency preparedness — all of these and many more owe their existence to the efforts of the "K's" of Kensington and other dedicated volunteer community groups. The Kensington Improvement Club, the Kensington Property Owners Association, the Kensington Community Council, and the Friends of the Library are four civic organizations that have played a major role in Kensington's development.

THE KENSINGTON IMPROVEMENT CLUB

The Kensington Improvement Club (KIC) was the first volunteer organization in Kensington. It was founded in 1921 when the community consisted of fewer than 300 residents. Street lights would not be installed for another year, and there was no local school. The purpose of the Club today remains the same as it was over 75 years ago: to promote and foster the general welfare of the community and to cooperate with county and local officials to attain needed improvements. The Club acts as a liaison with the County and represents community interests at both the local and county levels. The Club is administered by a board of 15 directors who meet monthly. Membership is open to all Kensington residents and property owners. Each fall the KIC sponsors a town hall meeting that also serves as a membership meeting, at which major issues concerning Kensington are discussed.

The KIC has been instrumental over the years in persuading the County Board of Supervisors to pass ordinances for the specific benefit of the Kensington community. In 1984 a Tree View Ordinance was adopted, and in 1987 an ordinance was passed placing restrictions on residential second units. In 1989, an ordinance establishing the Kensington Municipal Advisory Council was adopted to relieve the KIC zoning committee from acting as an unofficial advisory board to the County on zoning and variance applications in Kensington. In 1991 an ordinance was passed in cooperation with the Kensington Property Owners Association that established a Road Assessment District to reconstruct or repave every public road in Kensington. The KIC insisted the following statement be included in the ordinance: "After construction of all roadways is complete, the County of Contra Costa guarantees to continue fully funding a preventative maintenance program in Kensington that will prevent any roads from once again deteriorating to a condition that is not responsive to preventative maintenance. The post-repair maintenance program will require no further assessments or additional taxes on Kensington parcel owners" (Ordinance 92-46, Section 1, paragraph h).

Colusa Circle Traffic Island, 1997
Photo by Theodore Osmundson

In 1976, at the request of the KIC, the County Board of Supervisors, in cooperation with PG&E, undergrounded the utilities on Arlington Avenue and installed new electroliers. In the late 1980s the KIC persuaded the County to underground utilities at Colusa Circle and install a traffic island. The new island was landscaped in the spring of 1989 by KIC volunteers who, under the supervision of landscape architect Ted Osmundson, brought in new soil and planted trees and a colorful variety of plants, flowers, and ground covers. The KIC paid for the installation of an irrigation system and for the planting.

Until 1989, volunteers from the KIC Landscape Committee spent countless hours maintaining and planting the public areas in Kensington. However, when it became increasingly apparent that the work was beyond the capacity of KIC volunteers, the Club petitioned the Board of Supervisors to annex Kensington to the County Landscape District as Zone 21. In 1994-95 money from the District became available to begin renovating the five center strip islands on Arlington Avenue. Irrigation systems and plantings have been installed on two of the islands, and the three remaining islands will be renovated as funds become available.

Following the Loma Prieta earthquake, the Club published a detailed earthquake preparedness manual that was distributed to every household in Kensington, and a Neighborhood Block Emergency Preparedness program was organized, the forerunner of the current Neighborhood Emergency Assistance Team (NEAT) program.

Arlington Avenue South Median at Fire House, 1997
Photo by Theodore Osmundson

In 1977 the Club constructed a community signboard on the Arlington at the south entrance to Kensington, and in 1981 it constructed a kiosk for public notices in front of the drugstore. The Club maintains both the signboard and the kiosk. The Club has compiled and published two earlier editions of this book, in 1966 and 1978.

THE KENSINGTON PROPERTY OWNERS ASSOCIATION

The Kensington Property Owners Association (KPOA) is a non-profit organization formed in 1972 to collect and disseminate information on issues affecting property owners. Membership is open to all owners of real property in Kensington. The Association is governed by a board of no more than 15 directors who meet monthly. Annual dues are used for educational mailings and to promote civic projects.

The KPOA organized the Home Alert program, and has worked with other community groups to help solve problems facing the Fire and Police Districts following severe budget cuts. It initiated a study of the condition of roads in Kensington, which culminated in the Road Improvement Assessment District in 1992. In 1994 the KPOA carried out an audit of the Fire District, which led to a major reorganization of the Department. Along with the KIC and the KMAC, the KPOA nominates candidates for the KMAC and submits their names to the Board of Supervisors.

Every spring the KPOA holds an annual meeting that features speakers on important current topics affecting the Kensington community. The meeting announcement includes the Association's newsletter, a membership application, and a directory containing a map along with other community information.

THE KENSINGTON COMMUNITY COUNCIL AND THE PARK AND RECREATION PROGRAM

In the early depression days of the 1930s, when the population of Kensington was under 1,500, the Bay Association of Congregational Churches rented Fellowship House at 264 Arlington Avenue to provide church services and a Sunday School for the new community. When the Church agreed the building could also be used as a community center, Kensington residents began to address the need for a recreation program. Boy and Girl Scout troops were organized, dance classes started, and a children's play center opened. By the late 1930s, the building was in use for more than 100 meetings or classes a month.

In 1933 a Women's Society was formed, which was the forerunner of the Arlington Women's Club. In the early 1940s the first Kensington branch of the Contra Costa County library system established a lending stall at Fellowship House. When the church moved from Fellowship House into its new building on the corner of Arlington Avenue and Rincon Road in 1948, it promised to continue providing facilities for community groups and to support, encourage, and sponsor recreational activities. A Community Center Council was appointed to help define the relationship of the church with the various groups that were meeting there and to establish a more formal community recreation program. The first volunteer-directed summer program for children began in 1951 under the direction of Mrs. William Stiles. The program was so popular that spaces for classes were often filled on the first day of registration, and many applicants had to be turned away.

It soon became obvious that the rapidly expanding recreation program and the growing number of organizations in Kensington were outgrowing the facilities provided by the church. Across the street from the church, the Richmond School District owned approximately 18 acres of land between Arlington Avenue and Wildcat Canyon, which it had purchased in 1925 from Mrs. Ethel Smith to establish an elementary school. A large portion of this acreage remained unused. At the request of the Kensington Community Services District, the School District agreed to reserve all property not required by the elementary school

Volunteers Constructing Youth Hut, 1955

for future Kensington recreational facilities. In 1955, the Board of Education conveyed 1.22 acres to the KCSD for a community building, parking lot, and play area. Plans were immediately formulated for construction of the Youth Hut.

There was, however, no meaningful governmental agency that would offer assistance in either the planning or the financing of the building. The Youth Hut could become a reality only if it was a do-it-yourself project.

A committee headed by Mrs. Robley Berry undertook the job of raising funds to finance the building and recruit volunteer labor and donations of material for its construction. Community clubs and organizations held fundraisers, and Kensington contractor Arnold Lahti volunteered to oversee construction. Every weekend volunteers poured cement, hammered, nailed, painted, and landscaped the grounds while women set up a can-

Volunteers Landscaping Youth Hut, 1955

teen to provide sandwiches, cookies, and coffee to the workers. "Helpful" children acted as "go-fers." The Hut was completed in 1955 at the unbelievably low cost of $20,824.75. A dedication ceremony brought out hundreds of residents to view with pride what the many volunteers who so generously had contributed their time and effort had achieved at virtually no cost to the community. Today the building stands as a monument to what a community can accomplish through volunteer efforts.

The recreation program was moved from the Church into the new building, and by a vote of the electorate, the duties of the KCSD were expanded to assume responsibility for the Hut and for Parks and Recreation. In 1960 the Community Center Council was replaced by the Kensington Community Council (KCC), a non-profit volunteer corporation. Through a contract with the KCSD, the KCC formalized the recreation program. A recreation office was established in the Youth Hut Annex, a recreation coordinator was hired, and the program was expanded to include year-round classes for adults as well as children.

Tennis Courts at Kensington Park
Photo by Theodore Osmundson

The KCC is governed by a 20-member Board of Directors, and Board meetings are held monthly. Membership in the KCC is composed of community organizations approved by the Board, and membership meetings are held annually. The KCC is funded by contributions from the community solicited through an annual fund drive, class fees, and *Outlook* advertising.

After the Youth Hut was built, Kensington began to work toward creating a community park around the Hut to augment the limited recreational facilities already in place. In 1963 the KCSD and the Richmond Board of Education agreed on leasing arrangements for roughly 4.4 acres of unused school property adjacent to the library and Youth Hut at $1.00 per year. In 1965 the first plan for park development was drawn up. In 1966 Ted Osmundson volunteered to design and supervise the construction of an amphitheatre behind the Youth Hut. A tot lot and picnic area were completed by community volunteers between 1972 and 1978, and two tennis courts were added on land east of the library.

In 1987 the KCC remodeled and enlarged the Youth Hut using funds from a state grant and donations from individuals and organizations in Kensington. A conference room was opened for adult meetings, and in 1989 the building was renamed the Kensington Community Center to reflect the increased use of the building by all age groups.

Through a contract with the Kensington Community Services District, the KCC is now responsible for all of Kensington's recreational and educational programs. It also handles rental arrangements for private use of the Community Center. It runs the Kensington Summer Day Camp program and

KCC Adult Dance Class
Photo by Richard Edwards

sponsors two community events a year, the Spring Party and the Fall Parade and Open House. The Kensington After School Enrichment Program (KASEP) and the Home Alert Program also operate under the auspices of the KCC.

In addition, the KCC offers classes for adults, including exercise, art, dog training, and dance, as well as numerous classes for children including tennis and gymnastics. The Community Center is in use 119 hours a month for KCC classes and 175 hours per month for meetings of KCC member groups. The Center is also used for the KASEP program, which offers 44 classes to children ages five to twelve in a wide variety of subjects including pottery, sewing, carpentry, drawing, and sports. The KASEP is funded by donations and class fees. The popular Summer Day Camp program offers recreation and adventure opportunities throughout the summer for children six to twelve. A director, two counselors, and a "specialty consultant" are hired to work with the campers. Both the day camp and KASEP are extremely popular and have waiting lists. In addition, the Center is rented out for private use, such as wedding receptions and anniversary and graduation parties.

In April of 1992, the School District, on the

Kensington Community Center, 1997
Photo by Theodore Osmundson

verge of bankruptcy, declared all additional acres of school property not in use by the school as surplus. In two advisory votes on a property assessment in 1994 and 1995, Kensington voters gave approval to the KCSD to proceed with the purchase of all available acreage between Highland Boulevard and Arlington Avenue to be used for Kensington Park. Early in November 1994 a tentative real estate purchase and sale agreement for one parcel of 8.05 acres was signed between the School District and the KCSD pending a second advisory vote on a portion of the property. Escrow on the first parcel closed on June 22, 1995, and on the second parcel on January 26, 1996.

In May 1996 the KCSD appointed a 19-member Kensington Park Advisory Committee (KPAC) to create a master plan for the new park. The goals of the committee were to create a park that would balance the serene with the functional, build on the natural beauty and topography of the site, enhance its natural features including dramatic views of the Bay, increase functional spaces for recreation and education, and provide a focal point for community gatherings.

In 1997, the master plan for park development was presented to the KCSD and subsequently adopted. In 1998-99 all but two of the temporary buildings on the lower playground were demolished, the land was graded for a turf field, and utilities were undergrounded. The remodeling of Building E was started to provide for expansion of the recreation program.

THE KENSINGTON OUTLOOK

The Kensington *Outlook*, a periodical covering local issues and events, has been an integral part of community life in Kensington since 1944. The *Outlook* is published monthly ten times a year (December/January and July/August are combined issues) by the KCC. The newspaper reports on local government and civic affairs, provides publicity for the KCC and its member groups, and publicizes the KCC's programs such as community education/recreation classes, summer day camp, and the Kensington After School Enrichment Program. Other community news, including brief items about Kensington residents and their activities, is also featured.

The *Outlook* is funded by classified and display advertising and the KCC's annual fund drive and is mailed free of charge to every Kensington household and business in the commercial districts on Arlington and Colusa Avenues. It is also mailed, by request, to approximately 300 readers outside of Kensington and is available at Kensington businesses, the library, and the KCC office.

The *Outlook* has been described in the *West County Times* (February 1, 1992) as a "slick, forty-nine year old suburban-style newspaper, village crier, bulletin board and house organ for the Kensington Community Council." In his "Living in the Bay Area" column, real estate reporter Brad Inman called the *Outlook* "a snazzy little neighborhood newspaper" ("Kensington: An Island of Rationality," *San Francisco Examiner and Chronicle*, March 8, 1987).

The *Outlook* was originally created as the *Arlington Outlook* by Herbert Dimock, the first pastor of the Arlington Community Church. The Church published the periodical as a community service until 1960, at which time the KCC assumed responsibility for its publication. There are two versions of how the paper got its name. Some say the name was derived from the "outlook" over the Bay and San Francisco that Reverend Dimock had from his desk. Others claim the paper was created to provide an "outlook" on the progress and needs of the community. Both could be correct.

The staff, which is employed by the KCC, includes three part-time positions: editor, editorial assistant, and advertising manager. Marion Martin, who made the transition from the church to the KCC, was editor from 1960 until her retirement in 1978. She was succeeded by Diane Gossard. In 1983 Anna-Maria Hertzer was hired to fill the new position of assistant. Jean Cannon was advertising manager from 1976 until her retirement in 1998. She was replaced by Alma Key. Many volunteers currently contribute publicity about the activities of community organizations, and volunteers have served in various other capacities over the years.

The *Outlook's* production and distribution process has changed from time to time. In 1986 the editorial office moved from the editor's home to a workspace that the KCC rents. Commercial production services used in publishing the *Outlook* also change as new techniques are adopted. Addressing, which at one time was done in the church basement by volunteers, is currently handled by a commercial firm.

Prior to 1983-84 the *Outlook* was published from September to June. Since 1980 it has been published in an eight-page tabloid format (11x17 inches) with occasional 12-page issues. Earlier issues were somewhat smaller. Bound volumes from 1944 on are on file at the reference desk at the Kensington Library.

THE KENSINGTON LIBRARY AND
THE FRIENDS OF THE LIBRARY

No building in Kensington is more important to community life than the Kensington Library, a branch of the Contra Costa County Library System, located at 61 Arlington Avenue at the entrance to Kensington Park. The building itself, as well as many of its books and contents, stands as another monument to the spirit of volunteerism in Kensington. As early as 1922, residents approached the County about establishing a branch library in the community. When the Caudron family offered the use of a room in their house at 264 Arlington Avenue to house the library, the "Kensington Park Branch" was set up by Mrs. Alice G. Whitbeck, Contra Costa County's first librarian. Miss Catherine Caudron was appointed "custodian" of the initial collection of 50 books. At the end of the first year there was a book stock of 117.

Kensington Library, 1998
Photo by Theodore Osmundson

In 1925, the small library moved to the home of Miss Eleanor J. Loudon, who was appointed custodian. In 1931 the library moved into the Sulligar Real Estate Office in the neighborhood center, and in 1935 it was moved back into the Caudron home, which had become the Arlington Fellowship House.

In 1948, when Fellowship House was sold and no longer available for community use, the library was moved to a room provided in the new Arlington Community Church building. In 1952, as the library rapidly expanded in step with the growing population of Kensington, it was again moved to larger quarters in the basement of the church building.

Space was still inadequate for the growing library, and in 1959, the Kensington Improvement Club appointed a committee to form a Friends of the Kensington Library (FKL) group to study ways and means of permanently improving library facilities. The FKL was incorporated in November 1959 as a non-profit organization, and Jack Frankel was elected president. In 1960 the FKL compiled and mailed to every Kensington home a leaflet calling attention to the crowded library quarters and outlining the need for a public library building in the community. The Friends then spear-headed a drive to establish a County Library Service Area in Kensington to raise taxes to construct the building. At a hearing before the County Board of Supervisors on August 30, 1960, Service Area LIB 6 was established with no opposition.

The dream of a library building began to become a reality when the School District was persuaded to deed approximately 0.61 acres of unused school prop-erty to Contra Costa County for the sum of $1.00 as a site for the library. A gift of $9,000 offered by anonymous donors toward the construction of the building reflected how important a library was to Kensington residents. The firm of Barbachano, Ivanitsky, and Associates was appointed to design the building. Ulysses Barbachano, a Kensington resident, took a personal interest in designing a beautiful structure that fit into the natural topography of the hillside site. The building contract was awarded to J. Vila and Sons, and groundbreaking took place on February 2, 1965. The Friends of the Library, assisted by volunteers throughout the community, packed and moved books from the old library into the new building, and the new library opened at 12 noon on August 30, 1965. Circulation on the first day was 737, 130% higher than that of an average Monday. The first week's circu-lation was 2,538, 104% higher than the average weekly circulation during 1964-65. Dedication of the Kensington Public Library took place on September 19 with a program sponsored by the Friends of the Kensington Library.

Although the land on which the library stands belongs to the County, Kensington owns the building, having paid the $126,694 cost through a bond issue. Within five years the bonds were paid off, the mortgage was burned, and the Library Service District was dissolved.

Today the library's permanent collection includes 33,287 books, 85 periodicals, 900 audio-cassettes, 650 videos, and 40 compact discs. The library also lends its 16-mm audio visual projector to Kensington organizations. A Youth Service Librarian sched-ules story hours and other interesting programs for children. The spring of 1996 brought CARL, a colorful icon-oriented on-line catalogue system, and in the fall, hard-ware for a separate terminal for the Internet became available. Five stations are now set up for general use, including a Kids' Catalogue unit. The Internet is available on several of the machines; one terminal is dedicated solely to the Internet, and docents are available to instruct novices in its use. According to recent County records, library use by Kensington residents is 176% higher than the average use in Contra Costa County.

Interior of Kensington Library
Photo by Theodore Osmundson

The FKL continues to be an active organization, providing financial support to the library from membership dues and the proceeds from two yearly book sales plus an ongoing mini-sale in the library. The Friends purchase supplementary books, periodicals, music and video cassettes, tapes, magazine and newspaper subscriptions, compact disks, and other needed equipment for library use. Their contributions partially compensate for the recent series of state budgetary cuts to county libraries. The FKL also sponsors cultural events such as lecture series, author nights, photo contests, and children's programs. In addition, the Friends have purchased furniture, carpets, and other supplies for the building.

The FKL actively supports library legislation and recently established an in-library volunteer program that welcomes all interested Kensington participants. The FKL Board of Directors meets monthly at the library.

THE KENSINGTON BUSINESS AND PROFESSIONAL ASSOCIATION

The Kensington Business and Professional Association (KBPA) is dedicated to fostering positive community awareness of the over 150 Kensington businesses and professionals who consider themselves an integral part of the community. Recent goals include: (1) to establish a network of resources within the community to promote the Kensington spirit of self-sufficiency and to provide ready access to services; (2) to establish reciprocal relationships with neighboring communities; (3) to promote the positive attributes of Kensington with the intent of building identity and maintaining a strong sense of community; (4) to support projects that improve the quality of life in Kensington; and (5) to promote a sense of community responsibility among KBPA members.

The Association was started in 1977 in an effort to integrate the divergent business interests, merchants, professionals, artisans, and home-based operations in Kensington. Its hope is to translate local support of Kensington businesses into a more active role in improving the quality of life in Kensington through both individual and collective contributions to local events, education, and public works.

THE KENSINGTON LIONS CLUB

The Lions Club is a service organization that operates at both the local and international levels. The Kensington Lions obtained their formal charter in 1996 and are the Bay Area's newest Lions Club, though not the least active. The group is committed to both local community service and service to humanity internationally. On the local level the Club plans to become involved with projects benefiting the community such as beautification, public safety, education, and service to seniors and handicapped residents. The Club has sponsored a competition at Kensington Elementary School to collect used eyeglasses for the international "Lions in Sight" program; and in 1996 it hosted the first annual Colusa Circle Oktoberfest, a community "streetfair" featuring entertainment, family fun activities, and authentic German fare. Membership consists of local residents and business people who share a sincere desire to help less fortunate people in a spirit of fun and fellowship.

THE BLAKEMONT PROPERTY OWNERS ASSOCIATION

The Blakemont Property Owners Association is a non-profit mutual benefit corporation formed in 1984 to find an economically and technically feasible way to stop or reduce the creeping motion of the Blakemont Slide. The slide is a 19-acre pear-shaped swath of land that slopes downward from Arlington Avenue, through the Blake Estate, to Colusa Avenue in El Cerrito. Approximately 200 homes are located on the slide, which over the years has destroyed several houses, shifted foundations, buckled walls, cracked curbs, and burst sewer, gas, and water lines. The goal of the Association is to correct the underlying problems by forming a Geological Hazard Abatement District (GHAD), a governmental entity that has the ability to assess property owners within the boundaries of the slide to pay for a system of repairs to drain the hillside of excess water.

To date the Association has authorized and received a report from Seidelman Associates regarding the boundaries and characteristics of the slide, and a plan of control has been completed. The Association is now considering the pros and cons of a long term financial commitment to forming the GHAD and implementing the plan of control.

An annual membership meeting of the Association is required, and other meetings are called during the year on an "as needed" basis. A new Board was elected in 1997 to replace members of the original Board who had served since the Association was organized.

THE KENSINGTON AMATEUR RADIO OPERATORS

The Kensington Amateur Radio Operators (KARO) is a group of amateur radio operators who live in Kensington and have agreed to participate in the support of Kensington's emergency preparedness program. The operators have been operationally incorporated into the NEAT program and organizationally are a part of the Kensington Emergency Preparedness Council. KARO has volunteered its services to provide an emergency communication line to Kensington during a disaster when other lines of communication might not be operable.

KARO is currently meeting monthly while implementation plans are being drawn up. It later plans to meet on an ad hoc basis for training and drills, possibly two or three times a year. The group invites all Kensington residents to attend meetings; an amateur radio license is not a prerequisite. Citizens will be trained in the specific procedures that will be used in an emergency.

As part of its mission to kindle the interest of young participants in amateur radio, members of KARO recently sponsored a cooperative venture between Kensington fifth and sixth graders and those of Ohlone Elementary School in Hercules. Students were instructed in the basics of amateur radio operation and then given the opportunity to put their new-found knowledge to work by having fun talking with each other.

POLITICAL ORGANIZATIONS

THE KENSINGTON AREA REPUBLICAN WOMEN, FEDERATED

The Kensington Republican Women's Club was established in 1952 for the purpose of electing John Baldwin to Congress. The first president was Frances de Reynier. The name of the Club was later changed to the Kensington Area Republican Women, Federated, to reflect the growing membership outside Kensington's borders.

The purpose of the Club is to inform the membership on political issues as well as to promote and support Republican candidates for office. Candidates and other

Republican speakers are invited to address the Club at its monthly luncheon meetings held at the Mira Vista Country Club in El Cerrito. A news bulletin is mailed to members every month informing them of political developments as well as club affairs. A fashion show is held in the fall as a fundraiser.

The Club is affiliated with the California Federation of Republican Women and the National Federation of Republican Women. Membership is open to all registered Republican women. Spouses are eligible for associate membership.

THE EL CERRITO DEMOCRATIC CLUB

The El Cerrito Democratic Club was organized more than 40 years ago to provide a forum for area residents to discuss issues of local, national, and international importance and participate in a significant way in the election campaign process. The Club includes members from Kensington and other East Bay cities. It strives to promote the public welfare, to serve the principles of democracy, to fight unfairness and discrimination, and to do this with reason and with justice. In practice, the Club works to help elect Democratic candidates and encourage voter registration, voter education, and grass-roots lobbying. It works with other groups to promote local, state, and national issues the Club studies and supports.

The Club is chartered by the Democratic Central Committee of Contra Costa County and is affiliated with the California Democratic Council and the 14th Assembly District Committee. Meetings are held monthly in the Northminster Presbyterian Church in El Cerrito.

THE LEAGUE OF WOMEN VOTERS

The Kensington Unit of the League of Women Voters is part of the League of Women Voters of the Richmond Area, which in turn is affiliated with the League of Women Voters of California and of the United States. The League is a non-partisan political organization whose purpose is to encourage informed and active participation of citizens in government and to influence public policy through education and advocacy. The Kensington Unit keeps abreast of issues of concern to Kensington, as well as studying issues at all levels of government that affect this area. Position papers are published on many of these issues, all of which are based on careful studies. Membership is open to both men and women, and membership at the local level includes membership at all levels. Meetings are held monthly at members' homes.

SOCIAL AND CULTURAL ORGANIZATIONS

THE ARLINGTON WOMEN'S CLUB

The Arlington Women's Club is the oldest social organization in Kensington. It was founded in 1934 by John Gregg, the first Director of the Arlington Avenue Fellowship House, and his wife, who recognized the need for a "women's society" in the developing community of Kensington. The Club, initially called the Arlington Fellowship Women's Club, met at the Fellowship House at 264 Arlington Avenue. The word "fellowship" was dropped after the first year, and the Club moved its meeting room to the Arlington Community Church when the Fellowship House was sold in the 1940s.

General meetings of the Club, held monthly, feature speakers, musical programs, book reviews, fashion shows, teas, and luncheons. Special interest section meetings are held during the month and include bridge, needlework, armchair travel, fine arts, and garden sections. A special fundraiser is held in the spring, the proceeds of which support local projects or are donated to causes such as the Souper Center. Club membership is limited to 300.

THE KENSINGTON SENIORS

The Kensington Senior Activity Center is co-sponsored by the Arlington Community Church, the Richmond Older Adult School program, and the Bay Area Community Services Department. For the past 21 years the group has met every Thursday from 9:00 a.m. to 2:00 p.m. in the social hall of the Arlington Community Church. The Center is open to all those over 55 years of age in the larger Kensington community. Teams of volunteers contribute to the creative preparation and serving of healthful and delicious lunches. Traditionally, there is a first Thursday potluck lunch.

Programs provide a rich variety of presentations by experts and embrace the themes of the arts, nature, health, travel, history, life-planning, language classes, and holistic health. Guided meditation is offered by the minister. Day trips are occasionally scheduled. Massage therapy and blood pressure checks are regularly available. A Great Books discussion group meets monthly, and a computer-use class is available for all levels of ability.

All activities are designed to attract senior adults who enjoy meeting old friends as well as new people while participating in stimulating activities and learning new skills.

THE KENSINGTON SYMPHONY ORCHESTRA

The Kensington Symphony, founded in 1978, is an outgrowth of the former Contra Costa Symphony, which in turn became known as the Phoenix Orchestra when Robert Martin Kissel became conductor. The first rehearsal took place in a Berkeley garage in late 1977, and the first concert was presented at the Arlington Community Church in 1978. The orchestra was later invited to make its home at the Unitarian Church on Lawson Road, and because of its location, it was renamed the Kensington Symphony.

The Symphony is a non-profit, community-based group of approximately 60 musicians drawn from the greater Bay Area; it is considered an off-campus class of Contra Costa Community College. It provides classical music concerts at accessible East Bay locations at modest prices. Works are chosen to provide a variety of music styles, from baroque to modern, and selected to appeal to a wide audience while also providing a musical challenge for the orchestra. It features local artists and provides an opportunity for talented musicians, professional and non-professional alike, to continue to play fine music throughout their adult years. Lloyd Elliott is currently in his seventh season as Music Director and Conductor.

The Symphony sponsors an annual young soloist competition, the winner of which is invited to perform with the orchestra as a visiting artist during the spring season. Although the symphony is partially supported by Contra Costa College, the major portion of the operating budget is raised through ticket sales, advertising, and donations. The symphony now holds its concerts at the First Baptist Church just off Arlington Boulevard in Richmond.

YOUTH GROUPS

The Cub Scouts, Boy Scouts, Brownies, and Girl Scouts are all represented by Kensington troops. They meet, for the most part, in the Community Center or in private homes and are led by community volunteers. These young people have provided many hours of volunteer service to the community while earning service merit badges and satisfying Eagle Scout requirements. The cost of projects involving civic improvements is often underwritten by Kensington organizations.

The Girl Scouts collect clothes for Goodwill Industries, visit nursing homes, make toys for shelters, and participate in other projects that benefit the community. Boy Scouts have repaired park facilities, built recycling bins for the Community Center, and repositioned the blue fire hydrant markers that were removed during the street improvement program.

A creative project underwritten by the KIC and other organizations took place in 1992 when Eagle Scout candidate Jonathan Vlahos buried a time capsule on the grounds of the Community Center "to provide an historical perspective on Kensington to residents in the year 2043." Among items encased in the capsule were the 1978 KIC *Survey of Kensington*, copies of the *Outlook* and *San Francisco Chronicle*, old Kensington photographs, copies of interviews with community leaders, town hall meeting agendas, and the results of a statistical survey Jonathan took of Kensington residents. The letter enclosed in the capsule begins: "To Kensington Residents of 2043: Greetings from the 20th century. . . . you have before you a set of elements which was buried fifty years ago on a windy day in November, 1992." It ends, "We hope the Kensington we loved has not changed too much for the worse."

CHURCHES

THE ARLINGTON COMMUNITY CHURCH

The Arlington Community Church, one of the oldest institutions in Kensington, has played a significant role in the development of the community in addition to its religious role. The Church started with a Sunday School at the Fellowship House in 1932. Church services began in 1942. In 1944 the Church was recognized as an officially constituted Congregational Church by the Northern California Congregational Conference and, in 1960, the Church united with the United Church of Christ, a denomination rooted in Congregationalism. When it became clear that the many activities engendered by the Church had outgrown the space available in the Fellowship House and it was to be put up for sale, a location for a new building was found on the Arlington at the corner of Rincon Road, a site considered to be "way out" at the time. The cornerstone-laying ceremony for the new building, which included a nursery school playground to be constructed on land donated by Anson Blake to the south of the Church, took place in 1947. Anson Blake, one of the first directing committee members of the Fellowship House, was the featured speaker. He emphasized that the Church had pledged itself from the beginning to continue providing facilities for a community center program and to work with the community to implement a recreation program.

In 1952 the building was expanded to make room for the county library, a teenage canteen, and a chapel. In 1971, the Montessori School of Kensington was opened. Membership had grown from 85 in 1944 to 482 in 1956. To accommodate parking, the Church purchased the northern half of the lot across Arlington from the School District, and the Kensington Community Center Council purchased the southern half. The Lions Club held a benefit party in the Social Hall to help pay for paving the lot. A new sanctuary was built in 1960. Stained glass windows added to the beauty of the sanctuary.

The Church sponsors a wide variety of activities such as meditation workshops, prayer groups, social hours, potlucks, book discussions, men's and women's groups, and bible study. The Church has active junior and senior high groups that enjoy discussions, ski trips, camping, and other special events. It also supports social work outside the immediate area.

THE UNITARIAN UNIVERSALIST CHURCH OF BERKELEY

The Unitarian Universalist Church of Berkeley occupies a spectacular setting on top of Squirrel Hill in Kensington. It began as The First Unitarian Church of Berkeley in 1891 in the Oddfellows Hall in Berkeley. In 1898 the Church constructed its own building at Dana and Bancroft streets near the University of California, and in 1908 Bernard Maybeck, one of the 32 charter members of the church, designed the social hall adjoining the church. The Church moved to its Kensington location in 1961 when the University used its power of eminent domain to take over the Berkeley property.

The Church has become an integral part of community life in Kensington. In addition to Sunday services and religious education classes, the Church runs a steady stream of cultural and educational activities including drama, musical events, lectures, and seminars. It offers social gatherings and potluck suppers and is well known for its Christmas Bazaar. It serves as the headquarters for the Institute of Logotherapy, based on the teachings of Austrian psychiatrist Viktor Frankl and formerly headed by Frankl's leading American disciple, the late Joseph Fabry.

SOURCES

Friends of the Kensington Library, "Newsletter," August 1997.

From "Fellowship House to Community Church: Fifty Years of Growth," 1992 (author unknown).

Gossard, Diane. *The Kensington Outlook*.

Kensington Improvement Club. *A Survey of Kensington*, 1978.

Kensington Park Advisory Committee, "Kensington Park Master Plan," November, 1997.

Kensington Property Owners Association, "Study and Control of the Blakemont Slide," May 1997.

Library Link Supplement, "Kensington Library History," September 1965.

Vlahos, Jonathan, "Kensington Time Capsule Letter," November 1992.

SCHOOLS

5

Kensington is part of the West Contra Costa Unified School District (WCCUSD), formerly the Richmond Unified School District, which also includes El Cerrito, Richmond, El Sobrante, San Pablo, Pinole, and Hercules. The District is administered by the Superintendent of Schools. The Board of Education, made up of five members elected at large to four-year terms, sets policy. School enrollment boundaries have been readjusted through the years to provide for better integration of students. In time for the 1997-98 school year, with the assistance and advice of almost 900 parent volunteers throughout the district, the boundaries were again redrawn to enable students to attend schools closer to home.

In 1920, with a population of just 226, Kensington had no local school. Kensington children attended Oxford Elementary and Garfield Junior High in Berkeley, and either Berkeley High or the former University High School in Oakland. Following the disastrous Berkeley fire of 1923, many displaced homeowners moved to Kensington, and the need for a local school became more pressing. In 1925, two portable classrooms were brought in from

The Original Kensington School, c. 1925
Photo by Louis L. Stein

Richmond, and Kensington had its own elementary school. That same year, the Kensington Parent-Teacher Association (PTA) was organized.

By 1930 Kensington's population had increased to 1,430. The school population had outgrown the two portable classrooms, and a new two-story brick school was constructed on the "lower" school site. Every grade now had its own classroom. Classrooms had no electricity, but instead relied on natural light from the windows. Kensington's population continued to soar to over 6,000 by the late 1940s as young families moved into the community. To accommodate the increase in the school population, a much larger school (Kensington Hilltop Elementary) was built uphill from the lower school in 1949.

Kensington Elementary School, June 1945

The lower grades moved into the new school in the fall of 1950, while the upper grades continued in the brick school. In 1956 the brick building was demolished for seismic safety reasons, and all classes moved to the new school.

Education has always been of primary importance in Kensington, and Kensington Elementary School has enjoyed a reputation for excellence over the years. Student achievement is improved through excellent teaching and teamwork among students, parents, teachers, and principal. Kensington Elementary was one of 200 elementary schools in California to receive a 1993 California Distinguished Schools recognition award. It was second when considered for a National Blue Ribbon Award for Excellence in competition with approximately 100 other California Distinguished Schools.

Kensington Hilltop School, 1997
Photo by Theodore Osmundson

In the 1997-98 school year, a state-wide standard achievement test was given to all students, regardless of English proficiency. As one of 39 elementary schools in the district, Kensington achieved the highest scores in math, reading, language, and spelling. It seems reasonable to conclude that parent and community support are factors in the school's success.

Kensington School facilities include 23 regular classrooms, one special education classroom, a science lab, a computer lab, and a library. The school library holds approximately 7,747 volumes. The District's elementary school libraries are staffed by seven library assistants who divide their time among 39 schools. At Kensington, the assistant is on duty every Friday, doing mostly administrative work. The library is staffed every day by parent volunteers, and each class pays a weekly visit to the library. The computer lab has 20 computers connected to the Internet. In addition, every classroom has a computer with Internet capability.

Kensington School provides an enrichment program for all of its students. Every grade participates in a science laboratory program, as well as computer instruction and fine arts development, including music. The District provides instrumental music for the upper grades, while the Kensington Education Foundation funds vocal music instruction for the primary grades.

In 1997-98, the enrollment at Kensington School was 553. Sixty-four percent of the students lived in Kensington, while the remaining students came from all parts of the District. (Transfers to Kensington are granted by the District when space is available.) Under a state-subsidized program first implemented in the 1996-97 school year, grades K-3 were reduced to 20 students per class. Class sizes in the upper grades in the 1997-98 school year averaged 33 for fourth grade, 33 for fifth grade, and 30 for sixth grade.

In the 1997-98 school year, Kensington School had 21 Limited English Proficient (LEP) students, who spoke nine different languages. The following chart shows the ethnic distribution of the school in 1997-98.

1997-98 Ethnic Distribution (%)

	Kensington	WCCUSD
Native American	0.36	0.33
Asian	18.08	11.98
African American	6.33	35.22
Filipino	0.36	5.18
Hispanic	6.87	26.91
Pacific Islander	0.00	0.48
Caucasian	68.00	19.90

Source: WCCUSD Schools Report, 1997-98

Kensington has no secondary schools. Graduating sixth graders who live in Kensington are assigned to Portola Middle School in El Cerrito and then to El Cerrito High School. Kensington students may also apply to transfer to Adams Middle School, other schools outside the District, or private schools.

Four parent organizations support Kensington School: the Parent-Teacher Association (PTA), Dads' Club, Kensington Education Foundation (KEF), and Site Council.

THE PTA

The PTA, which was organized at Kensington School in 1925, has a long history of service to the faculty, students, and parent community of the school. In the school year 1994-95, the PTA logged a total of 13,000 parent volunteer hours. Through a network of room parents, it provides direct support to classroom activities. The enrichment programs that the PTA adds to the curriculum include the Royal Reader program, the Young Audiences program, the Reflections Art program, and the annual Science Fair. It has assisted with the development of a disaster plan for the school and purchased emergency and first aid supplies. The PTA also publishes the *Kenvue*, a monthly newsletter sent to all parents. It co-produces the annual Kensington School Carnival with the Dads' Club and assists the Kensington Education Foundation (KEF) with the annual Garden Party, the school's major fundraising event.

Kensington School Graduating Class, 1945
Photo by Louis L. Stein

THE DADS' CLUB

The Kensington Dads' Club is a service organization whose aim is to involve fathers in school activities. It was established in 1946 and became a California corporation in 1958. The members of the Club offer their labor and expertise in response to the school's never-ending needs for repairs or improvement that the School District cannot provide.

Significant Dads' Club projects have included purchasing and installing playground equipment in the kindergarten play area as well as in the playground for older children, window replacement, and major earthquake preparedness work. The Club holds annual parent-son and parent-daughter nights, co-produces the annual School Carnival with the PTA, and assists the KEF with its annual fundraiser, the Garden Party.

Kensington School, c. 1945
Photo by Louis L. Stein

THE KENSINGTON EDUCATION FOUNDATION

The KEF was established in 1984 as an incorporated non-profit organization. Its purpose is to raise funds in addition to the annual $25,000 to which the PTA is restricted under its national and state rules. Its Board of Directors consists of parents, the principal of the school, and the presidents of the PTA and Dads' Club. The substantial funds raised by the Foundation have been used for various enrichment programs such as art, music, and science. The KEF also contributes to the purchase of library books and computers. The principal and faculty submit a proposed budget for "extras" to the Foundation.

Kensington School Class Photo, 1957
Photo by Richard Edwards

THE SITE COUNCIL

Every school in the state is required by law to have a Site Council. At Kensington School, it is composed of the principal, the secretary, three faculty members, and five parents. The Council's functions are to decide how to spend funds allocated to the school by the State School Improvement Program and to address concerns at the school site.

PRIVATE SCHOOLS

ARLINGTON PRESCHOOL

52 Arlington Avenue (Arlington Community Church)

The Arlington Preschool was established in 1968 by the Arlington Community Church as a drop-in child care center. It was licensed as a preschool in 1972. The school is open from 9:00 a.m. to 4:00 p.m. and accepts children from age two years and nine months to six years. Children are encouraged to function in group settings through music, cooking, movement, and "circle time." The low adult-child ratio allows for individual attention to each child.

CLAREMONT DAY NURSERIES

1550 Oak View Avenue

The Kensington campus of the Claremont Day Nurseries has been at its present location for about 35 years; other branches are in Berkeley and Oakland. There are six teachers and one housekeeper. The school opens at 7:00 a.m. and is licensed for 65 children, ages two to seven. The two to five age group is divided into four classes. Day care is offered for kindergarten children from 11:30 a.m. to 6:00 p.m. and for first graders after their school hours. Ballet, gymnastics, and swimming are offered.

GOLDEN GATE APPLE SCHOOL

379 Colusa Avenue

The Golden Gate Apple School was founded in 1976 and has been at its Kensington location since 1984. It offers individualized programs for students from kindergarten through 12th grade. Forty-five to fifty students are enrolled in the program, some of whom are ahead of grade level and some of whom need to catch up. The Kensington Teachers Institute, which instructs teachers from various communities in the use of phonics, is also part of the program. Monthly seminars on the Spalding method of phonics are held for teachers, parents, and others who are interested. Tutoring is offered for all ages.

KENSINGTON NURSERY SCHOOL AND DAY CARE

52 Arlington Avenue (Arlington Community Church)

The Kensington Nursery School is a parent cooperative founded in 1940 by a group of Kensington parents under the sponsorship of the Works Project Administration (WPA). Thirty-five children were enrolled at that time, and staff was paid by the WPA. In 1942, the WPA withdrew its funds, and the school became a parent cooperative. It has been at its present location since 1943. The school is accredited by the National Academy of Early Childhood Programs. It offers a morning nursery school program with parent participation and an afternoon program without parent participation. It admits children age two years and nine months through kindergarten age. The school offers an escort service for children in the morning kindergarten program at Kensington School so that students can participate in the afternoon session at the nursery school. An enrollment of 28 in the morning program and 26 in the afternoon program is considered ideal. The school is open from 7:30 a.m. to 6:00 pm.

MONTESSORI FAMILY SCHOOL

1 Lawson Road (Unitarian Universalist Church)

At the beginning of the century, Dr. Maria Montessori, a physician, originated a school of thought that won many adherents and revolutionized teaching. Dr. Montessori believed that there are many ways to learn and that children learn best by doing, rather than by memorization. Her method encourages children to explore new concepts from many angles. World peace is the goal of the Montessori method. Montessori schools can be found throughout the world.

The Montessori Family School was established in Berkeley in 1981. The primary school moved to its present location in 1996. It accepts children from first through sixth grades. Preschool children remain at the Berkeley location.

GROWING LIGHT MONTESSORI SCHOOL

52 Arlington Avenue (Arlington Community Church)

The Growing Light Montessori School adheres to the Montessori philosophy. The emphasis is on building self-confidence, promoting language skills, expressing feelings, and teaching independence. The School offers programs for toddlers ages two to three, preschoolers ages three to five, and elementary school students from kindergarten to third grade.

THE NEIGHBORHOOD SCHOOL

59 Arlington Avenue (Community Center Annex)

The Neighborhood School was established in 1979 as a preschool under the auspices of the Kensington Community Council recreation program. In 1985, the Kensington Community Services District and the KCC required that the school obtain a license from the State of California. This was accomplished in 1989, and the school now operates independently.

The school has an enrollment of approximately 85 children. It offers toddler classes for two year olds, preschool classes for three to five year olds, and before and after school daycare for elementary school children from kindergarten through fourth grade. It provides pickup services for Kensington School children from kindergarten through fourth grade, and escorts them to the Kensington After School Enrichment Program (KASEP) classes at the Community Center.

SKYTOWN PARENT COOPERATIVE PRESCHOOL
1 Lawson Road (Unitarian Universalist Church)

Skytown has been in operation since the mid 1960s. It is unique among preschools because its toddler program accepts children as young as 18 months. The program operates under the direct supervision of a fully qualified preschool teacher. It is a morning program with the option for extended care. The maximum class size is 12 children with an adult to child ratio of one to three.

The preschool program is for children three years of age through kindergarten. It is supervised by the school's director, who has a BS in child development. The adult to child ratio is approximately one to four or five.

The cooperative structure of Skytown promotes parent involvement in all aspects of the school and offers families a choice of four types of participation ranging from full to minimal.

There is a walkover service for Kensington School kindergarten children to Skytown for afternoon care.

SOURCES

Blackman, Anna and Kosel, Cathie, "WCCUSD Schools Report, Kensington Hilltop School, 1997-98."

Brochures from private schools.

Loring, Marianne, Interviews with Judith Kantor, Principal of Kensington School, and Carole Travers, Secretary, September 1998. Telephone interviews with personnel of private schools, summer 1998.

West County Times, February 1, 1992.

THE PEOPLE OF KENSINGTON

6

The information in this chapter about the people of Kensington is derived from the U.S. Census reports, County records, and the 1995 KIC Questionnaire. The figures from these several sources are not wholly comparable. The Census gives the most reliable information on what it asks, while the KIC Questionnaire can only report the sentiments of the respondents. In the fall of 1995 the Improvement Club sent out questionnaires to all 2,316 households in the community. During the following months, the Club received 1,408 replies from 1,108 households (there was space for two sets of answers), a good response for a mailing of this kind. But this response does not constitute a valid sampling of Kensington residents or all variations of opinion in Kensington. Clearly those residents who were most interested in community action were more likely to have replied. Nevertheless, the responses are of special interest to those charting the future of our community.

In the Census of 1990, the most recent for which figures are available, Kensington's population was just under 5,000 (4,974). This was a decline of nearly 20% in the three decades following 1960. Since the total number of households remained roughly constant at about 2,200 over this period, the decline clearly reflects the aging of the community and the presence of fewer children — except when the grandchildren come to visit! In 1990 only 405 Kensington households had children in residence, fewer than one in five.

Kensington is a community of primarily single-family homes occupied by their owners. The 1978 KIC Survey reported only 68 multi-family residence parcels containing 142 units. The 1990 Census counted 2,251 housing units in Kensington, of which 2,197 were occupied. Of the occupied units, 1,878 were owner occupied (85.5%) and 319 were renter occupied (14.5%). Kensington is a community of older homes with few remaining vacant lots for new housing. Nine out of ten (89%) of the 2,197 occupied housing units were built prior to 1960. Only slightly more than a third (37%) were constructed prior to 1940. However, by 1960 Kensington was nearly fully built; between 1960 and 1990 only 246 (and in the decade of the '80s only 37) new houses were built, just 11% of the whole housing stock in that 30-year period. Currently only a handful of buildable lots are vacant.

In this stable community, houses are no longer very densely inhabited. In 1990, most housing units in Kensington were occupied by only one or two persons. About a quarter were occupied by one person; somewhat fewer than half (44%) were occupied by two persons; about one in six (16%) were occupied by three persons; and about the same proportion (15%) held four or more persons. Only 83 units out of the over 2,000 homes were occupied by five or more persons. The average number of people per housing unit was 2.26, down from three persons in 1960 and 2.52 persons in 1975. In 1990 most houses in Kensington had from two to four bedrooms, about a quarter had two bedrooms, roughly two in five (43%) had three bedrooms, and one in five (21%) had four bedrooms. Just one house in 20 had one bedroom, while one in 30 (3.4%) had five or more. The average number of bedrooms was nearly three per housing unit.

The value of Kensington housing has increased dramatically since 1960, when the average value of a Kensington house was $23,300. By 1990 the mean value of owner occupied housing units in Kensington had risen to $340,348, nearly 15 times higher than in 1960, and five times higher than the roughly comparable median value of $62,467 in 1970. In 1990, of the 17 unincorporated areas in Contra Costa County, only Blackhawk at $566,626 and Alamo at $499,986 had higher median values. In 1990, 20% of Kensington houses had a value of less than $250,000; another 20% had a value ranging from $250,000 to $300,000; 37% had a value ranging from $300,000 to $400,000; 15% had a value ranging from $400,000 to $500,000; and 8% had a value exceeding $500,000. Moreover, the value of most houses in Kensington has continued to grow over the eight years since 1990.

As we have noted, Kensington is a relatively stable community. In 1990 over three out of five residents had lived here for at least 15 years, and over a third had lived here for 25 years or more. In the 1995 Questionnaire, only 10% of the respondents reported that they had lived in Kensington for less than two years. The stability of the community not only adds to Kensington's attractiveness as a place to live, it also partly accounts for Kensington's ability to provide local control of its essential services.

While there is limited bus service in Kensington, most residents in these hills need cars to get to work on time and to transport packages and shopping bags. As a result there are many more automobiles than houses, and in 1990 there were four cars for every five residents. In 1990 more than three-quarters of living units in Kensington had one or two vehicles, and another one in five homes had three or more vehicles. Only one in twenty households in Kensington did not own a car or other vehicle. In 1990 the mean number of vehicles per housing unit was 1.78, and the total number of vehicles in Kensington was nearly 4,000 (3,915), for a population then of just under 5,000. The average commute to work was just under half an hour, while nearly one in five had a commute of longer than three-quarters of an hour. Of those 1995 KIC Questionnaire respondents working away from home, 82.5% went to work by car while 4.5% used the bus and 10% used BART. Of those respondents commuting to work, 59% commuted 10 miles or less; 25% commuted between 11 and 20 miles; and 16% commuted over 20 miles.

In the 1990 Census, of 5,000 inhabitants, more than two-thirds of the adults (69%) were gainfully employed, and of those, fewer than one in seven (14%) worked at home, while the rest worked away from home, most outside of Kensington. In the 1995 Questionnaire, 57% of respondents reported they were gainfully employed, while fully 40% were retired. Of those employed, nearly half (49%) worked at their homes either full or part-time, most of them (40%) part-time. While the Questionnaire cannot claim to be a representative sample, it is likely that the proportion of Kensington residents working at their homes is distinctly higher today than it was in 1990. In this special and highly educated community we may be seeing the early impact of the revolution in electronic communications and information technology.

The 1990 Census described the people of Kensington as relatively affluent, older, and well educated. Moreover, the relatively older population continues to age. In 1970 only 13% of Kensington residents were over 65; by 1990 that figure had grown to 23%, compared to only 14.4% for all of Contra Costa County. (In the 1995 Questionnaire, 37% of the 1,408 respondents were over 65.) In 1990 the median age of Kensington residents was 44.6, as compared with 34 for Contra Costa County and 31.5 for the state as a whole. As the population ages, it declines in numbers (though occupying the same number of houses) as children leave home and the average size of the households falls — from 3.0 in 1960 to 2.26 in 1990. As mentioned earlier, this has led to a substantial decline in the population of Kensington in recent years.

With respect to income, in 1990 the median household income in Kensington was $61,330, higher than all other unincorporated areas in Contra Costa County except Discovery Bay, at $65,494, Alamo, at $93,089, and Blackhawk, at $129,135.

Another demographic statistic undergoing change concerns population diversity. In 1960, 98.8% of Kensington's residents were white; by 1990 that percentage dropped to 86.8, thereby raising the percentage of its non-white residents to 13.2%. Slightly more than 16% of the population is foreign born; 40.1% were born in states other than California, most of them coming from the Midwest.

In May 1996 there were 4,163 registered voters in Kensington. Of this number, 63.6% were registered Democrats, 21.6% Republicans, and 14.8% "other" or "declined to state." By contrast, in the mid-1970s, 55.9% of registered voters were Democrats, 38.6% Republicans, and 5.5% "other" or "declined to state."

Kensington is one of the most highly educated communities in the nation. An article published in the *San Francisco Chronicle* in the spring of 1998 reported that of all the communities in the United States with a population of greater than 3,500, Kensington ranked eleventh in the level of higher education achieved by its citizens. In 1990 the Census showed that seven out of ten Kensington residents over 18 had a college degree, and more than a third (37%) had a postgraduate degree. The 1995 Questionnaire showed that more than 90% of adult respondents had a college degree, and nearly two-thirds had done some post-graduate work, though the Questionnaire did not ask what number held higher degrees. In 1990 roughly one resident in five (1,021 out of 4,974) was enrolled in school at some level — about two in five of those 1,021 were enrolled in higher education, nearly half in elementary school or secondary school, and a little over one in ten in pre-primary school. Among the residents are many teachers and professors, lawyers, doctors, professionals of every kind, business leaders, and over the years, even several Nobel Prize winners. Surrounded by professors and colleges and universities, Kensington's children tend to go to college. In the July/August 1998 *Outlook* article about the graduating high school seniors from Kensington in 1998, 21 out of 23 were enrolled in college the following fall, leaving two who had not yet decided.

SATISFACTION WITH KENSINGTON'S GOVERNMENT AND SERVICES

A cluster of questions in the KIC Questionnaire allows us to explore respondents' varying degrees of satisfaction with Kensington's community services and special districts. The central fact about Kensington politically is that it is a small unincorporated area. Many of its services are provided by two special service districts (Kensington Fire Protection District and Kensington Police Protection and Community Services District, referred to as KCSD), administered by unpaid but elected Boards. Part of the support for these and other

Table 1

SATISFACTION WITH PUBLIC SERVICES IN KENSINGTON
Comparison of Answers to Questions 19 and 28

QUESTION 19					
Degree of Satisfaction With	Very Satisfied	Satisfied	Neutral	Dissatisfied	Very Dissatisfied	Other or No Answer
KCSD (a)	43%	41%	7%	2.3%	.7%	6%
KFPD (b)	44.6%	36%	9%	2%	.4%	8%
KMAC (c)	12.3%	18%	38.3%	2.9%	2.2%	26.3%
School (d)	20.1%	19%	27%	2.3%	1.1%	30.5%
WCCUSD (e)	2.2%	5.6%	30.3%	14.1%	15.1%	32.7%
Safety (f)	26.8%	46.4%	10.6%	4.5%	1.1%	10.6%
Roads (g)	18.9%	43%	15.8%	11%	2.5%	8.8%
Volunteer Organizations (h)	22.5%	35%	24%	2.5%	1.6%	14.5%
QUESTION 28					
Special Districts and Taxes	15%	41.2%	16.5%	11.4%	5.5%	10.4%

See Appendix

KEY TO ABBREVIATIONS

a   Kensington Community Services District (KCSD)
b   Kensington Fire Protection District (KFPD)
c   Kensington Municipal Advisory Council (KMAC)
d   Kensington Elementary School
e   West Contra Costa Unified School District (WCCUSD)
f   Kensington Safety
g   Kensington Roads
h   Kensington Volunteer Organizations

services comes from property taxes; part derives from the special taxes and bonds that local residents vote for when they tax themselves to increase the levels of services.

A key question in the Questionnaire asked whether respondents were satisfied with Kensington's arrangements for raising funds in order to maintain or improve services (see Appendix, Question 28). They were given five choices: very satisfied, satisfied, neutral, dissatisfied, and very dissatisfied.

On the whole, respondents indicated a broad pattern of satisfaction with the way Kensington supports its public services. Moreover, even among the small number of respondents who indicated they were dissatisfied or very dissatisfied with Kensington's arrangements for taxation (16.9%), nonetheless well over half expressed satisfaction with almost every aspect of Kensington's services provided by special districts (Question 19). Therefore, even those relatively few people who are dissatisfied with Kensington's form of government are still likely to be satisfied with the quality of the public services delivered through that form of government.

The reference to Kensington's form of taxation to support its special districts in Question 28 refers to Kensington's central and distinct characteristic, that it is an unincorporated area, unlike its neighboring communities. This means Kensington has chosen not to burden itself with the bureaucracy and expense of governmental machinery that incorporated towns and cities require.

It is a reasonable inference that the more satisfied people are with Kensington's local services, and with its way of supporting those services, the more satisfied they are with Kensington as an unincorporated area. Further evidence is provided in recent decades by Kensington voters, who have rejected proposals to change this governmental arrangement four times, twice to make Kensington a city, and twice to incorporate with neighboring El Cerrito.

In summary, we find that people who are happy about a key aspect of our community — its being an unincorporated area — are also on the whole happy about the way their services are provided. The pattern of responses to the Questionnaire as a whole shows a broadly satisfied community, but also one that indicates room for further improvement. This finding may help explain the resistance of Kensington's voters to changing their form of government, whatever their degree of dissatisfaction with any particular service might be.

The broad pattern of satisfaction with Kensington's public services among the respondents to the 1995 Questionnaire shows itself in this summary of Table 1:

Of the 1,408 respondents, over half (56%) expressed satisfaction or strong satisfaction; one in six respondents (17%) was dissatisfied or strongly dissatisfied; while about a quarter (26%) were either neutral or declined to answer (Question 28). Adding together only those who expressed any degree of either satisfaction or dissatisfaction with Kensington's services and omitting "neutral" and "other" categories, over three-quarters (77%) expressed satisfaction or strong satisfaction with this system, while fewer than a quarter were dissatisfied. Indeed, only 7% of respondents who held any opinions expressed strong dissatisfaction.

Table 1 shows that those Kensington residents who responded to the Questionnaire were generally satisfied with the provision of local services, with the important exception of the West Contra Costa Unified School District, which provides public schools for Kensington residents (Question 19). Nearly a third of our respondents indicated a degree of dissatisfaction with the school district, and nearly another third were neutral; fewer than 8% expressed satisfaction with that institution. Apart from these attitudes toward the public schools, the overall finding of the Questionnaire is that residents of Kensington are broadly satisfied with the quality of public services provided by the community.

SOURCES

Contra Costa County Planning Department.

Contra Costa County Community Development Department.

Kensington Improvement Club. *A Survey of Kensington*, 1966.

Kensington Improvement Club. *A Survey of Kensington*, 1978.

Kensington Improvement Club. 1995 Kensington Questionnaire.

U.S. Bureau of the Census.

Kensington Improvement Club Board of Directors, March 2000
Photo by Paul Lettieri

CONCLUSION

7

This concludes our story of the history and development of Kensington. We have traced the land from its earliest occupancy by small peaceful Indian tribes through the period of Spanish expeditions and Mexican land grants. We continued the story to show how the southeast corner of Victor Castro's Rancho San Pablo grant was, upon his death, divided into eight major subdivisions, a small portion of which was then developed into the community of Kensington. We described how Kensington's first landowners — the dairymen —

fought to keep their independence in 1917 by refusing to be incorporated into the city of El Cerrito, and how, as Kensington grew, its citizenry molded the new community into a closely knit self-reliant village.

This is a history of both continuity and change. At the beginning of the millennium we find Kensington to be a community with a thriving social and political infrastructure that rises above the conventional by effectively linking the traditions of rural America with the perspectives and technologies of the urban life

View to San Francisco from Kensington
Photo by Paul Lettieri

around it. Those who live here consider themselves fortunate to be located in such an extraordinarily beautiful part of the world and to have had the privilege of managing their own community life to such a high degree.

As we enter the millennium, we reflect on the past, but we must also plan for the future; and as we do so, we find the future of Kensington is not without challenges. Growth has been stabilized, and all properties zoned for business are occupied. The possibility of continued expansion through vertical growth and an increase in construction of second units could jeopardize the safety of our already congested streets, making parking more difficult and obstructing views. Unfortunately, the community has no authority to enforce zoning regulations, but must rely on the County. In addition, the threat of wildfire from the interface with the East Bay Regional Parks and the rumblings of the Hayward Fault under our homes give rise to ever-present thoughts of emergency preparedness.

The greatest challenge to Kensington, however, now and in the future, is the serious consequence of any decrease in the involvement of its citizens in community affairs. Kensington is an unincorporated, do-it-yourself community with a rich history of independence. It prides itself and depends upon the spirit of volunteerism exhibited by its residents. This spirit of volunteerism is the common thread which, the reader will find, runs throughout the story of Kensington. It is the glue that holds the community together and makes it possible for its unincorporated status to work to the benefit of its residents.

As we look back over this story of Kensington, we are reminded of the great debt we owe the many volunteers in the past who gave their time and expertise to help shape our community. It now becomes our responsibility to continue this commitment into the future. Failing that, Kensington's future may indeed be compromised.

It is our hope that this book will encourage all Kensington residents to support their community by attending District and town hall meetings and by offering their services on community boards and committees. The Fire and Police Districts, the Municipal Advisory Council, the Kensington Community Council, the Improvement Club, the Property Owners Association, and Kensington Park all need volunteer help. Kensington is a challenging place in which to live. May we continue to meet its challenges with enthusiasm and vigor. The future of Kensington depends on a strong commitment by its citizens.

Committee at Work on the Book, 1999
Natalie Salsig, Paul Lettieri, Marianne Loring, Katherine Trow

APPENDIX

1995 Kensington Survey

Questionnaire

The Kensington Improvement Club is updating a "Survey of Kensington," originally published in 1966 and 1978, in preparation for a 1996 revised edition containing information about the history, land use, population characteristics, habits and needs of the community. This booklet will be available to residents of Kensington. (Free to K.I.C. members) Answers will be kept confidential, and only a summary of the results will be published. Please return the completed questionnaire in the self-addressed envelope by December 1, 1995 *even if you do not wish to become a member of the Improvement Club.*

Use a pencil. Please mark only one circle/box for each question. Answer separately for each adult. Extra questionnaires are available at the Kensington Library for additional adults in your household.

Adult 1	Adult 2	The Questions
a b ☐ ☐	a b ○ ○	1. Are you a) male? b) female?
a b c ☐ ☐ ☐	a b c ○ ○ ○	2. What is your age? a) 18-40 yrs b) 41-65 c) over 65
a b c d e ☐ ☐ ☐ ☐ ☐	a b c d e ○ ○ ○ ○ ○	3. How long have you lived in Kensington? a) Less than 2 yrs b) 3 to 10 yrs c) 11 to 17 yrs d) 18-29 yrs e) over 29 yrs
a b c d e ☐ ☐ ☐ ☐ ☐	a b c d e ○ ○ ○ ○ ○	4. How long have you lived in the Bay Area? a) Less than 2 yrs. b) 3 to 10 yrs c) 11 to 17 yrs d) 18-29 yrs e) over 29 yrs
a b c d e ☐ ☐ ☐ ☐ ☐	a b c d e ○ ○ ○ ○ ○	5. Where were you born? a) U.S. (what state?_____) b) Europe c) Asia d) Central or Latin America e) Elsewhere (_____)
a b c ☐ ☐ ☐	a b c ○ ○ ○	6. What is your employment status? a) employed full time b) employed part time c) retired
a b c ☐ ☐ ☐	a b c ○ ○ ○	7. Do you work at home? a) full time b) part time c) not at all
a b c d e ☐ ☐ ☐ ☐ ☐	a b c d e ○ ○ ○ ○ ○	8. If you work away from home, do you get there by a) car b) bus c) BART d) walk e) bicycle
a b c d e ☐ ☐ ☐ ☐ ☐	a b c d e ○ ○ ○ ○ ○	9. If you carry on a business or professional service in Kensington, what percentage of your customers or clients live in Kensington? a) Less than 10% b) 10-30% c) 30-50% d) 50-75% e) over 75%
a b c d e ☐ ☐ ☐ ☐ ☐	a b c d e ○ ○ ○ ○ ○	10. How many miles do you commute to work one way? a)under 3 miles b) 3-6 c) 7-10 d) 11-20 e) over 20 miles
Fill in brackets please ➜		11. What are the ages of additional persons living in your household? How many are under 5 [__] 6 to 11 [__] 12 to 17 [__] 18 to 22 [__] 23 to 30 [__] 31-55 [__] 56-70 [__] 71 and over [_]
a b c d ☐ ☐ ☐ ☐	a b c d ○ ○ ○ ○	12. How many years of schooling have you completed? a) 8 years or less b) 12 yrs c) 16 yrs d) over 16 yrs

Adult 1   **Adult 2**

Fill in brackets please →

13. Of your children living at home, how many attend
WCCUSD public school [__]   Other public school [__]
private school [__]   parochial school? [__]

a b c d e   a b c d e
□ □ □ □ □   ○ ○ ○ ○ ○

14. How many automobiles (or other vehicles requiring parking space
such as trailers, boats, etc.) are parked regularly at your address?
a) 1 b) 2 c) 3 d) 4 e) 5 or more

a b   a b
□ □   ○ ○

15. Do you own the house in which you live in Kensington? a) yes b) no

a b   a b
□ □   ○ ○

16. If yes, do you rent any portion to unrelated persons? a) yes b) no

a b c d e   a b c d e
□ □ □ □ □   ○ ○ ○ ○ ○

17. How many bedrooms are in your house
a) 1 b) 2 c) 3 d) 4 e) 5 or more

a b c d   a b c d
□ □ □ □   ○ ○ ○ ○

18. Approximately how much of your day-to-day shopping (groceries,
gas, etc.) do you do in Kensington?
a) less than 10% b) 10-30% c) 30-50% d) more than 50%

19. How do you feel about the following aspects of Kensington?
a) very satisfied b) satisfied c) neutral d) dissatisfied e) very dissatisfied

a b c d e   a b c d e
□ □ □ □ □   ○ ○ ○ ○ ○   19a—Kensington Community Service District
                                   (Police, Recreation, Garbage)
□ □ □ □ □   ○ ○ ○ ○ ○   19b—Kensington Fire District
                                   (Fire and Emergency Medical Response)
□ □ □ □ □   ○ ○ ○ ○ ○   19c—Kensington Municipal Advisory Council
□ □ □ □ □   ○ ○ ○ ○ ○   19d—Kensington Hilltop School
□ □ □ □ □   ○ ○ ○ ○ ○   19e—WCCUSD secondary schools
□ □ □ □ □   ○ ○ ○ ○ ○   19f—Safety and security (including traffic safety)
□ □ □ □ □   ○ ○ ○ ○ ○   19g—Kensington Roads
□ □ □ □ □   ○ ○ ○ ○ ○   19h—Kensington's voluntary organizations, such as Kensington
Community Council, Kensington Improvement Club, Kensington
Property Owners Association

a b c   a b c
□ □ □   ○ ○ ○

20. How concerned are you about potential damage from earthquakes?
a) very concerned b) somewhat c) not at all concerned

a b c   a b c
□ □ □   ○ ○ ○

21. How concerned are you about potential damage from fire?
a) very concerned b) somewhat c) not at all concerned

a b   a b
□ □   ○ ○

22. Have you made any preparations for earthquake survival?
a) yes b) no

a b   a b
□ □   ○ ○

23. Have you joined any neighborhood groups concerned with disaster
preparedness? a) yes b) no

Adult 1	Adult 2	
a b	a b	24. Would you be interested in joining such a neighborhood group? a) yes b) no
☐ ☐	○ ○	
a b c d	a b c d	25. How much emphasis should the community place on efforts to develop plans to underground utility lines? a) a great deal b) some c) little d) none
☐ ☐ ☐ ☐	○ ○ ○ ○	
a b c	a b c	26. Would you be willing to pay between $1,000 and $5,000 for electric utility undergrounding? a) yes b) no c) we already have it
☐ ☐ ☐	○ ○ ○	
a b c d	a b c d	27. How much emphasis should the community place on efforts to develop evacuation plans in case of fire or earthquake? a) a great deal b) some c) little d) none
☐ ☐ ☐ ☐	○ ○ ○ ○	
a b c d e	a b c d e	28. Because Kensington's basic services are provided by special districts, we are periodically asked to vote new taxes in order to maintain or improve our level of public services (police, fire, roads, etc.) How do you rate your satisfaction with this current arrangement? a) very satisfied b) satisfied c) neutral d) dissatisfied e) very dissatisfied
☐ ☐ ☐ ☐ ☐	○ ○ ○ ○ ○	

For question 28, please elaborate on the source of your satisfaction or dissatisfaction on the the lines below.

_____

_____

_____

_____

29. What project or activities do you suggest the Improvement Club sponsor? _____

_____

_____

30. If you were asked to state your image of Kensington in a short phrase, what would it be?

_____

_____

31. What aspects of Kensington would you like to see improved?

_____

_____

Please use the back of this sheet for any further comments.
Thank you for your participation in the 1995 Kensington Survey.